WHAT I WANT TO BE WHEN THEY GROW UP

WHAT I WANT TO BE
WHEN THEY GROW UP
by Michael Fry

Andrews and McMeel
A Universal Press Syndicate Company
Kansas City

Committed is distributed internationally by United Feature Syndicate, Inc.

 For information write Andrews and McMeel, a Universal Press Syndicate Company, 4900 Main Street, Kansas City, Missouri 64112.

ISBN: 0-8362-1308-4

Library of Congress Catalog Card Number: 95-80752

Committed and *Over the Hedge* may be viewed on the World Wide Web:
http://www.unitedmedia.com

Send Michael Fry e-mail at:
MichaelFry@aol.com

For Kim:

Who works so hard
so I can hardly work.

Foreword

The way I see it, when it comes to raising kids, you can read Benjamin Spock, T. Berry Brazelton, Penelope Leach, all manner of What-To-Expect-Books—or you can read Michael Fry. Now that his cartoons have been assembled in this handy collection, the choice seems even easier. Every parent knows that child rearing is irrational, exhausting, and absurdly, even relentlessly funny, yet Fry is the only expert to address this reality. Where, for instance, does Leach discuss integrating the Pizza Man into the extended family portrait? Does Brazelton offer solace from the horror of headless Barbies? Do you ever really know what to expect from leaking toilets, past due life insurance bills, or a daughter who, in spite of all teaching to the contrary, still wants to be a princess when she grows up?

Unlike the rest of the experts, Michael Fry offers a perfect snapshot of parenthood in the nineties, in which we are our parents—coming to terms with ear infections, peanut butter, and semi-detached dads—and we are not. (How **did** they make it, you may have wondered, without Gap Kids, recycling, or Sunday drives on the Information Superhighway?) In *What I Want to Be When THEY Grow Up*, Fry, himself a happily married father of two strangely familiar young girls, shows us the American family at its self-deprecating best, valiant procreators in this age of two paycheck families, political correctness, and diminished expectations. It's all here, from Prozac to recycling to sexually confused GI Joes to yogurt filled piñatas to a visit from the Working-Mom Ghost of Christmas Past ("... and then in 1989 you forgot to string the popcorn and cranberries ..."). In Fry's affectionate yet devilishly satiric world, mothers are harried but loving ("If you don't stop that, I'm going to spank your inner child," one warns), fathers are distracted but loving ("I see your dad made your lunch today," one teacher notes of a child's midday meal of Pepsi and pizza), and, thankfully, just about everyone hates Barney. In the gentlest way, Fry tells us to give it a rest—that it's okay to give in to the minivan and the sugar-coated cereal, to give up on fantasies of flat stomachs, thin thighs or of ever finding the remote control. "Smoking or Non-smoking?" Fry's maitre d' asks a hungry couple. "Drinking or Non-drinking ... fun or no fun?"

Fun, of course, is what this book is full of. One thing the child care experts invariably fail to address is the absolute joy of living with small children, no matter how trying they can be. That of course, is the entire subtext of Fry's book. It's probably best appreciated at a 3 A.M. feeding, or while stuck in traffic with two children and a broken air conditioner, but any time will do.

Mimi Swartz
Senior Editor, *Texas Monthly*

FORGET IT,
I'LL CATCH THE
CLIFF NOTE.

PIZZA, SODA, COOKIES, PIXIE STICKS... THE FOUR MAJOR FOOD GROUPS.
I SEE YOUR DAD MADE YOUR LUNCH AGAIN...
DAY CARE
PEPS
OREOS
PIZZA
MICHAEL FRY

"A MAN IS SO IN THE WAY IN THE HOUSE."
-ELIZABETH GASKILL-
NEVERMIND... I'VE GOT IT.

KEN... DON'T WORRY... SHE'LL BE BACK... SHE LEFT HER GOLD LAMÉ PANTSUIT!
THELMA & LOUISE & BARBIE
...YOU SURE YOU DON'T WANT TO TAKE MY PINK VAN?
MICHAEL FRY

"LESS IS MORE."
-LUDWIG MIES VAN DER ROHE-
CABLE READY
IT'S IN OUR PRICE RANGE...
FOR SALE BY OWNER
MICHAEL FRY

"WE ARE GIVEN CHILDREN TO TEST US AND MAKE US MORE SPIRITUAL."
- GEORGE F. WILL

"IT IS TELEVISION'S PRIMARY DAMAGE THAT IT PROVIDES TEN MILLION CHILDREN WITH THE SAME FANTASY, READY-MADE AND ON A PLATTER."

—MARYA MANNES—

"PARENTS ARE THE LAST PEOPLE ON EARTH WHO SHOULD HAVE CHILDREN."
—SAMUEL BUTLER—
DOG IN THE HAT
GREEN EGGS AND HAM?
DR. SPOCK, NOT DR. SEUSS!!
MICHAEL FRY

EARTH DOG.
DOES BARBIE WEAR BIRKENSTOCKS?
KIDS SANDAL SALE
MICHAEL FRY

"IT'S NOT A LIE, IT'S A TERMINOLOGICAL INEXACTITUDE."
—ALEXANDER HAIG—
TRUTH
THAT'S BOVINE DIGESTIVE BYPRODUCT!
CLASSIC LIES
BEFORE KIDS
THE CHECK IS IN THE MAIL...
AFTER KIDS
MGRHMPH...
THE CHECK IS IN MY DAUGHTER...
MICHAEL FRY

"I HATE HOUSEWORK! YOU MAKE THE BEDS, YOU DO THE DISHES—AND SIX MONTHS LATER YOU HAVE TO START ALL OVER AGAIN." —JOAN RIVERS—
INVASION OF THE BODY SNATCHERS
HERE, LET ME DO THAT.
WHO ARE YOU?
MICHAEL FRY

"PARENTS ARE NOT QUITE INTERESTED IN JUSTICE, THEY ARE INTERESTED IN QUIET." -BILL COSBY

IF CHILDREN WERE DESIGNED WITH PARENTS IN MIND...

CLICK

Z. Z.

MICHAEL FRY

SOON TO BE
A DAVID LYNCH
FILM.

DOG.
BIG DOG
LITTLE DOG.
BLACK AND WHITE DOGS.
DO YOU LIKE MY HAT?
I DO NOT LIKE YOUR HAT.
GOOD BYE.
GOOD BYE.
GO, DOG. GO!
"GO, DOG, GO!": ZEN MASTERPIECE
MICHAEL FRY

Content: sugar.
Sugar
NUKES
MICHAEL FRY

"THEY'RE
GR-R-REAT!"
-TONY THE TIGER-

"I BASE MOST OF MY FASHION TASTE ON WHAT DOESN'T ITCH."
-GILDA RADNER-

"WOMEN SHOULD TRY TO INCREASE THEIR SIZE... ...BECAUSE THE BIGGER WE ARE THE MORE SPACE WE TAKE UP, AND THE MORE WE'LL HAVE TO BE RECKONED WITH."
-ROSEANNE ARNOLD-

"A MEDIUM, SO CALLED BECAUSE IT IS NEITHER RARE NOR WELL DONE."
-ERNIE KOVACS-

NO UTENSIL SECTION
SNARF SNARF SNARF SNARF
SCREAMING OR NON-SCREAMING?
Menu
MICHAEL FRY

SQUEAK SQUEAK SQUEAK
Oops!
PEDIATRICIAN HUMOR
COULD YOU STEP BACK?... YOU'RE IN MY LIGHT.
MICHAEL FRY

BOB
BOX-O PINK WINE
BEST WHEN CHILLED TO 32° AND SERVED AS POPSICLES
THE DAYS OF WINE AND OATMEAL
HOW LONG UNTIL WE CAN GO SHOPPING?
I GET PAID AT THE END OF THE WEEK.
BOX-O WHITE WINE
MICHAEL FRY

"HITCH YOUR WAGON TO A STAR."
-RALPH WALDO EMERSON-
UH, OH...
CADIO FLYER
AND WHAT DO WE WANT TO BE WHEN WE GROW UP?
DANCER... WRITER...
TATER TOT.
MICHAEL FRY

HELLO, MY NAME IS BOB. I'M COMPLETLY NORMAL AND WELL ADJUSTED AND I HAVE NEVER BEEN A VICTIM OF ANYTHING
GOODBYE, BOB!

CHILDREN'S SUPPORT GROUPS
HELLO, MY NAME IS TRACY AND I'M A PICKAHOLIC.
HELLO, TRACY!
MICHAEL FRY

MISSING SOMETHING?
HOFFA
MICHAEL FRY

AH... THERE'S MY COPY OF "NO BAD DOGS."
MGRMPHXLT...

THIS WAS BARNEY IN HIS ACTION-ADVENTURE PHASE, BEFORE THE DYE-JOB AND THE ORTHODONTIA...
T REX
MICHAEL FRY

I HATE YOU... YOU HATE ME... I DON'T WANT TO BE A CANINE CANAPE!

" I'M GROWING OLDER, BUT NOT UP."
-JIMMY BUFFET-

RECOVERING
adult
MICHAEL FRY

'DO YOU KNOW WHO MADE YOU?' 'NOBODY AS I KNOWS ON,' SAID THE CHILD, WITH A SHORT LAUGH... 'I 'SPECT I GROW'D.'
-HARRIET BEECHER STOWE-
Poof
GOD'S MARKETING DEPT.
CHILDREN
POSITIVE
CUTE
NEGATIVE
PRONE TO SPILLS
UNCOORDINATED
HIGH VOLUME
EXPENSIVE
FUNNY ODOR
EAR INFECTIONS
HARD TO DISCIPLINE
LACK OF BLADD CONTROL
BUT, WE'LL MAKE THEM REALLY, REALLY CUTE!
MICHAEL FRY

"AND ALL THE LITTLE GIRLS CRIED, 'BOO HOO, WE WANT OUR APPENDIX OUT, TOO!'"
-LUDWIG BEMELMANS-
IF DOLLS COULD TALK
WANNA SEE MY SCAR AGAIN?
SHUT UP, MADELINE!!
MICHAEL FRY

I'M SEEING HIM, BE ME,... BE HIM, BE ME, HIM, ME, ME, HIM... I'VE GOT A HEADACHE.
"MY-SIZE" BOB
EXISTENTIAL "MY-SIZE BARBIE"
SHE'S WEARING MY CLOTHES, I'M WEARING HER CLOTHES, SHE LOOKS LIKE ME... I LOOK LIKE HER. BARBIE IS ME. I AM BARBIE. THERE IS NO BARBIE. THERE IS NO ME. WE ARE ONE. WE ARE BARBIE.
UH, OH...
SIZE BARBIE
DRESS HER IN YOUR OWN CLOTHES
YOU WEAR HERS
MICHAEL FRY

"A PHYSICIAN CAN BURY HIS MISTAKES, BUT THE ARCHITECT CAN ONLY ADVISE HIS CLIENTS TO PLANT VINES."
-FRANK LLOYD WRIGHT-
AND YOU THOUGHT WE COULDN'T AFFORD A NEW ADDITION.
LEGO BLOCKS
MICHAEL FRY

QUALITY TIME

MICHAEL FRY

WHAT'S WRONG?
I FEEL WORTHLESS.
I FORGOT TO FOLLOW UP ON A LEAD WITH BIOTECH AND LOST THE ACCOUNT TO D.B.S.
IT'S JUST ONE ACCOUNT.
SOMEHOW THAT DOESN'T MAKE ME FEEL ANY BETTER.
MAYBE IF YOU WERE MORE ORGANIZED.
?!@¢$ MEN.
I DON'T WANT SOLUTIONS!! I WANT SYMPATHY!!
YOU WANT ME TO TELL YOU I KNOW HOW YOU FEEL? I **DON'T** KNOW HOW YOU FEEL!
THEN, **LIE!!**
I KNOW HOW YOU FEEL.
YOU CAN'T POSSIBLY KNOW HOW I FEEL.
YOU KNOW, YOU NEVER REALLY HAVE ENOUGH CONFUSION IN A MARRIAGE.
MICHAEL FRY

I WANT TO BE A PRINCESS WHEN I GROW UP.
REALLY?
WILL WORK FOR SMALL-MEDIUM SIZED FIEFDOM
YOU KNOW, THEY LIVE IN SMELLY DARK CASTLES.
THEY'RE CONSTANTLY IN DISTRESS, COMPLETELY DEPENDENT ON IRON-CLAD MEN TO SAVE THEM.
WOULDN'T YOU LIKE TO BE A HIGH-POWERED ASSISTANT SALES MANAGER LIKE YOUR MOM?
DO THEY LIVE HAPPILY EVER AFTER?
...PLUMBERS... ...PODIATRISTS... ...PRINCESSES: SEE OPPORTUNITIES; FAIRY TALE.
WANT ADS
MICHAEL FRY

WE'VE GOT TERMITES IN THE LATTICE-WORK AGAIN.
DON'T FORGET TO CUT THE LIFE INSURANCE A CHECK TOMORROW.
WE NEED TO GET ZELDA'S SOCIAL SECURITY NUMBER FOR THE TAX RETURN.
THE TIRES NEED TO BE ROTATED ON THE EXPLORER AGAIN.
THE DOWNSTAIRS TOILET'S LEAKING AGAIN.
AGAIN?
AGAIN.
PECK
MICHAEL FRY
PARTY ON HON.
PARTY ON, DEAR.

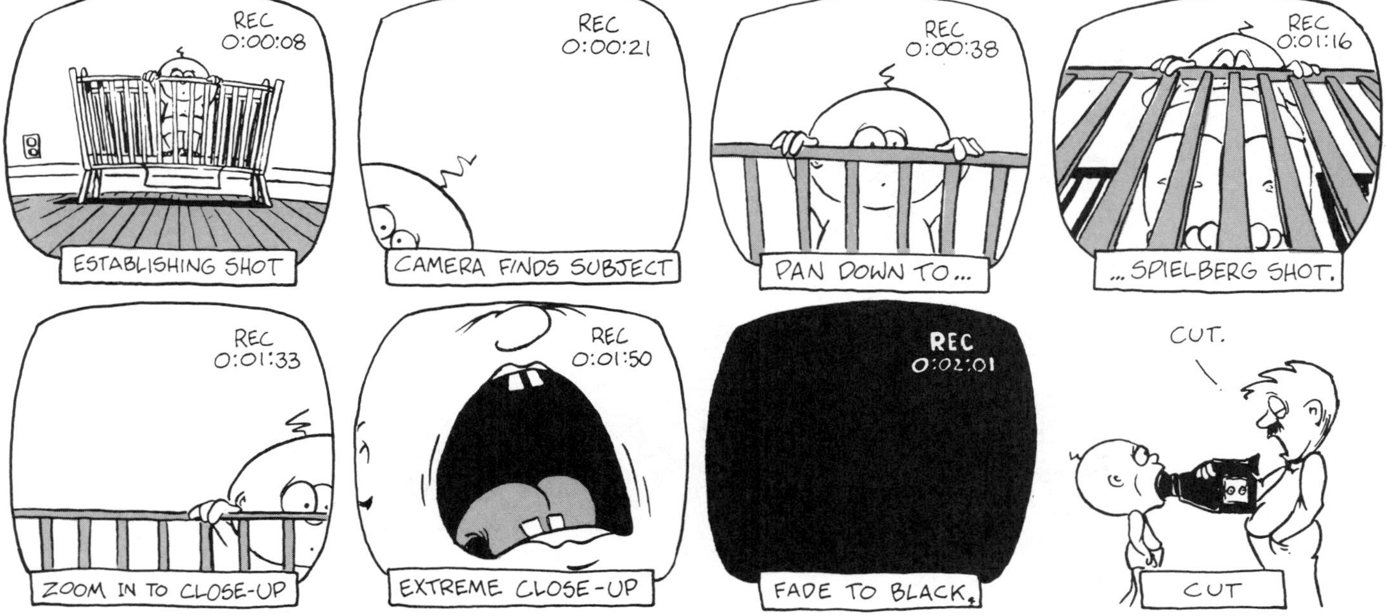

REC 0:00:08
ESTABLISHING SHOT
REC 0:00:21
CAMERA FINDS SUBJECT
REC 0:00:38
PAN DOWN TO...
REC 0:01:16
...SPIELBERG SHOT.
REC 0:01:33
ZOOM IN TO CLOSE-UP
REC 0:01:50
EXTREME CLOSE-UP
REC 0:02:01
FADE TO BLACK.
CUT.
CUT

HI! HOW WAS TRACY'S DAY?
SHORT PEOPLE DAY CARE
WONDERFUL!... WE STARTED WITH PHONETIC CONCEPTS BY MEDITATING ON THE LETTER "Y."
...THEN WE HAD THE SELF-ESTEEM HOUR WHERE WE ALL DISCOVERED HOW PERFECT OUR TOE-NAILS WERE.
DURING PUPPET OPERA WE ALL SANG THE KITTY ARIA IN THE ORIGINAL ITALIAN FROM MOZART'S RARELY PERFORMED "LE WHISKERS."
AFTER LUNCH WE HELD SUBLIMINAL NAP THERAPY WHILE STEPHEN HAWKING'S COMPUTER-GENERATED VOICE READ, "A BRIEF HISTORY OF TIME."
A BRIEF HISTORY OF TIME
AFTER NAP WE FINISHED WITH A ROUSING NON-COMPETITIVE MATCH OF ROGO—THE ANCIENT PRECURSER OF RED ROVER- RED ROVER.
WOW!
WE HAD A PRODUCTIVE AND STIMULATING DAY
HEY KIDDO! I HEARD YOU HAD A BIG DAY!
YEAH!
I SHOT MILK OUT MY NOSE AND INTO CHARLIE'S EGG SALAD.
COOL!
MICHAEL FRY

Day Care Drop-Off
CAN YOU SPOT THE WORKING PARENTS?
$300 CASHMERE TURTLENECK FROM COMPLETELY INSANE GRANDMOTHER
SEAS: CHOPPY WAVES: 5-7 FT.
CRAYOLA EYE SHADOW
"LITTLE MERMAID" BARRETTE
LIPSTICK APPLIED IN TRANSIT
J. CREW JACKET THAT LOOKED A LOT SLIMMER ON THE MODEL.
MURINE: GETS THE BLOOD OUT
THE MUCOUS KID
[NOT PICTURED] VICTORIA SECRET BLACK LACE MERRY WIDOW (BOTTOM OF DRAWER- OUT OF UNDERWEAR)
THREE-YEAR SUPPLY OF EGG CARTONS FOR ENDLESS ART PROJECT FROM HELL.
HAIR
HAIR
NO HAIR
DAY CARE PROFIT CENTER
$5 PER MINUTE LATE FEE
5:30 PICK-UP
1% HEARING LOSS FOR EACH LISTENING OF BARNEY'S "I LOVE YOU" SONG.
J. CREW SPORT COAT THAT LOOKED A LOT SLIMMER ON THE MODEL.
SHOW AND TELL AND SCREAM AND RUN.
[NOT PICTURED] FRED OF HOLLYWOOD "STUD THONG" (BOTTOM OF DRAWER- OUT OF UNDERWEAR)
MICHAEL FRY

BODY LANGUAGE
I'M HAVING A GOOD HAIR YEAR.
I'M HAVING GAS.
I'VE GOT THAT LOVIN' FEELIN'.
I'VE GOT THAT CHAFIN' FEELIN'.
THESE ARE THE BEST DAYS OF MY LIFE.
THESE ARE THE BEST DAYS OF MY LIFE.
GOTTA SING... GOTTA DANCE...
GOTTA RALPH.
I'M INTO SILVERWARE.
I'M INTO EVENING WEAR.
I'M NOT YAWNING.
I'M NOT SLEEPING.
MICHAEL FRY

"IF EVERYONE ON EARTH JUST STOPPED BREATHING FOR AN HOUR, THE GREENHOUSE EFFECT WOULD NO LONGER BE A PROBLEM." -JERRY ADLER-

"THE ONLY THING THAT SEEMS ETERNAL AND NATURAL IN MOTHERHOOD IS AMBIVALENCE."
-JANE LAZZARE-

"HEH-HEH
HEH-HEH
HEH-HEH."
-BUTT-HEAD-

I COULD WRITE THAT!

BOOM! BOOM! BOOM! BOOM!
THEY JUST KEEP GOING AND GOING AND GOING...
WHERE KIDS GET THEIR ENERGY
Z. Z. Z. Z Z
MICHAEL FRY

AHHHHHHHHHHHHHHHHHHH
A WORD IN EDGEWISE
WHY? NOW! BUT, I WANNA NO? MORE! CAN I? PLEEEASE! IN A MINUTE? TODAY!
HI
WHAT?
GAH!! BAH...BLEAH MGHMPH!! RGLPHXT!!... WHINE! WAH! MA-MA! DA-DA!!!
MICHAEL FRY

INSULIN ANYONE?
HAPPY BIRTHDAY
MORE CAKE AND ICE CREAM?
NO THANK YOU.
MICHAEL FRY

"I AM AT TWO WITH NATURE."
-WOODY ALLEN-
INDOOR PLUMBING
BOB
MOTHER NATURE
FATHER NATURE
I'LL SEE YOUR CHEERIO AND RAISE YOU A FRUIT LOOP.
TOO SWEET FOR MY BLOOD.
MICHAEL FRY

"TELL ME WHAT YOU EAT AND I'LL TELL YOU WHO YOU ARE."
-ANTHELME BRILLAT-SAVARIN

HEY!

AYEEEEEEEEEE
SIGMUND VOID
An Interpretation of SCREAMS
SIBLING RIVALRY?
CHEERIO UP NOSE.
MICHAEL FRY

" SOMETIMES A CIGAR IS JUST A CIGAR."
- SIGMUND FREUD-
URP...
GREEN

POPPED IN 100% YAK FAT
MUNCH
MUNCH
MUNCH
BOB

CHEZ DAD
DINNER?
WHAT?! POPCORN'S A VEGETABLE!
MICHAEL FRY

HEY! I WANTED THE EARLY COOL ELVIS, NOT THE LATER BLOATED ELVIS!
THE FIRST HAIRCUT
DON'T FORGET TO LAYER IT.
MICHAEL FRY

ALL MICROBES HALF PRICE! MUTANT STRAINS GET IN FREE!!
PARRRTY!
A CHILD'S INNER EAR
CLUB INFECTION
NO ANTI-BIOTICS
The Bacteriums
HELD OVER 33RD BIG WEEK
MICHAEL FRY

PUSH DOWN WHILE TURNING?
OREOS
THE TERRIBLE TWO'S
I'M SORRY, YOU CAN'T CRUMBLE OREOS INTO YOUR OATMEAL.
WAHHHH
THE TERRIBLE THIRTY-TWO'S
EITHER OF YOU!
MICHAEL FRY

"ONCE MORE UNTO THE BREACH, DEAR FRIENDS, ONCE MORE;...
-SHAKESPEARE- HENRY V, III:1
I AM NOT A FRENCH POODLE!
WHERE CHILDREN'S GAMES COME FROM
RED ROVER RED ROVER SEND THE FRENCH RIGHT OVER.
MICHAEL FRY

"EVEN WHEN FRESHLY WASHED AND RELIEVED OF ALL OBVIOUS CONFECTIONS, CHILDREN TEND TO BE STICKY." -FRAN LEBOWITZ-

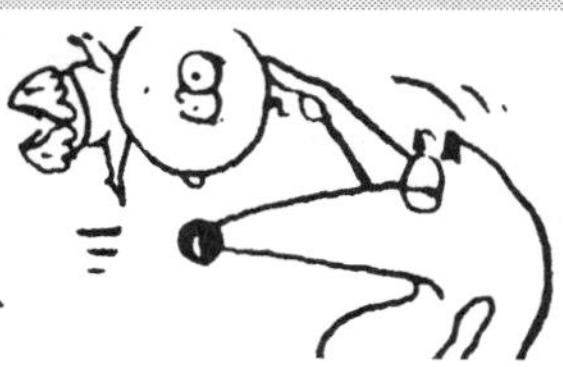

THE PERFECT CHILD IS:...

...QUIET

...POLITE

...CLEAN

...NEAT

...SELF-RELIANT

...EASY TO PLEASE

...LOYAL

...INEXPENSIVE

...A GOLDFISH..

MICHAEL FRY

GOOOD KITTIES...
GOOOOD KITTIES...
BE COOL.

"THE DOG KING."

GRRRRR..

FAIRY TALES FOR DOGS

...AND THEN THE BIG BAD DOG HUFFED AND PUFFED AND SCRATCHED AND SNIFFED AND TOOK A NAP AND THEN FORGOT WHERE HE WAS...

THE 3 Little Porkers

IF CLONING WERE READILY AVAILABLE...
WOMEN
MEN
MORE TROLLING FOR CARP AFTER THESE MESSAGES
MICHAEL FRY
NEXT ON THE DOG CHANNEL, "FETCH," THE LATEST DOCUMENTARY FROM KEN BURNS.

AT LEAST SHE HAS A WINDOW SEAT
PORT-A-PET

THE SCREAMING SECTION
MICHAEL FRY

"PIZZA IS THICKER THAN WATER."

— MODERN PROVERB —

"IF YOU HAVE NEVER BEEN HATED BY YOUR CHILD, YOU HAVE NEVER BEEN A PARENT."
-BETTE DAVIS-
?
SNIFF
FANTASY PARENT
ALTHOUGH WE SYMPATHIZE WITH YOUR NEED FOR A PET YAK WE FEEL THAT OUR AVAILABLE SPACE DOESN'T BLAH, BLAH, BLAH, BLAH, BLAH...
REAL PARENT
NO.
MICHAEL FRY

"THERE IS NO FINER INVESTMENT THEN PUTTING MILK INTO BABIES."
-WINSTON CHURCHILL-
HONEY, WE MUTATED THE KID!
HORMONE? OR HORMONE-FREE?
MICHAEL FRY

'THE SIMPSONS' WAS ANIMATED IN FRONT OF A LIVE AUDIENCE OF PEOPLE WITH REALLY LONG ATTENTION SPANS.
THE PARENTING POLICE
WE'VE HAD A COMPLAINT YOU'VE BEEN SPENDING YOUR QUALITY TIME WATCHING "THE SIMPSONS" WITH YOUR KIDS.
MICHAEL FRY

"IN ORDER TO INFLUENCE A CHILD, ONE MUST BE CAREFUL TO NOT BE THAT CHILD'S PARENT OR GRANDPARENT."
-DON MARQUIS-
...OR DOG.
RADIO FLYER
HAVE YOU FIGURED OUT HOW TO GET THEM TO CLEAN THEIR ROOMS?
I HAVEN'T EVEN FOUND THE RIGHT CHAPTER YET!
WHY CHILDREN DON'T COME WITH AN INSTRUCTION MANUAL
MICHAEL FRY

HOUSECLEANING
SHAKE
SHAKE
BOING
PING

WORKING MOM FANTASY #1
WE'RE THE OBSESSIVE/COMPULSIVE CLEANING FAIRIES. WE'VE COME TO STERILIZE YOUR HOUSE!
OUT! DARN SPOT!
MICHAEL FRY

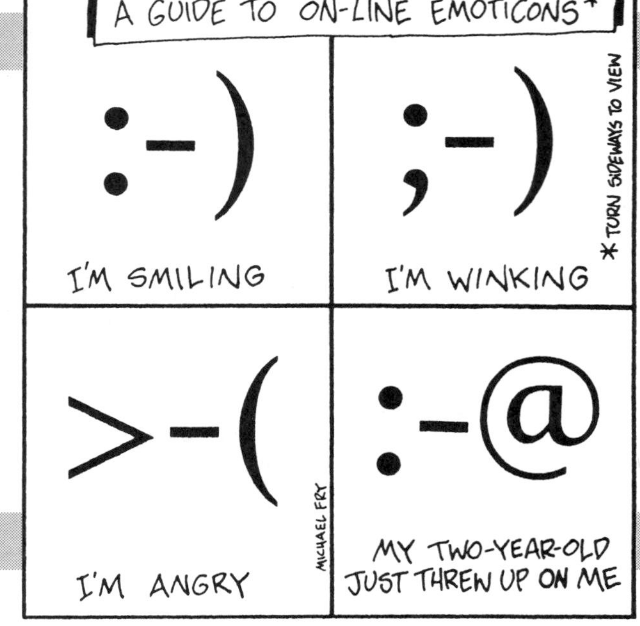
A GUIDE TO ON-LINE EMOTICONS*
:-)
I'M SMILING
;-)
I'M WINKING
* TURN SIDEWAYS TO VIEW
>-(
I'M ANGRY
:-@
MY TWO-YEAR-OLD JUST THREW UP ON ME
MICHAEL FRY

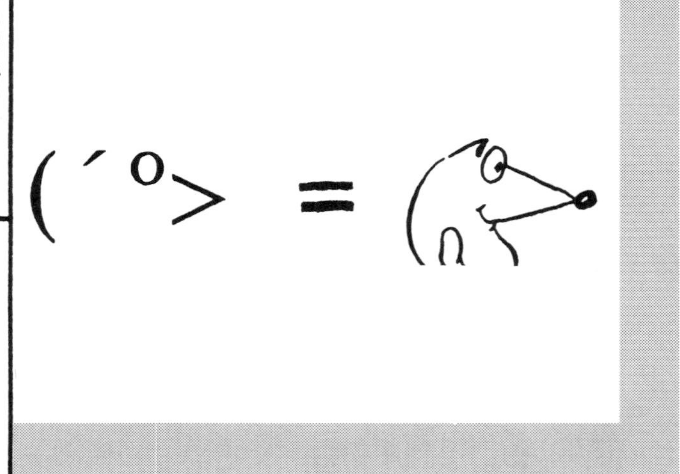
(´o> =

"NO MATTER HOW OLD A MOTHER IS, SHE WATCHES HER MIDDLE-AGED CHILDREN FOR SIGNS OF IMPROVEMENT."

-FLORIDA SCOTT MAXWELL-

YOU COULD BE LAZIER IF YOU TRIED

MOM?

"BY WORKING FAITHFULLY EIGHT HOURS A DAY YOU MAY EVENTUALLY GET TO WORK TWELVE HOURS A DAY." -ROBERT FROST-
WORKS NO HOURS A DAY
SNORT ...
MOMMY, WHAT DO YOU DO AT WORK ALL DAY?
I SUPERVISE A STAFF OF SALES REPS AND MANAGE A DISTRIBUTION NETWORK FOR THE SOUTHWEST REGION.
MICHAEL FRY
I MAKE MONEY FOR TOYS AND DINNER.
HEY!

DISOBEDIENCE CLASSES
TIP#38: FETCH THE PAPER... SHRED IT TO BITS... THEN THEY CAN'T HIT YOU WITH IT!
PARENTING CLASSES
DISCIPLINE WORKS... BUT BE FIRM, AND BE CONSISTENT.
CHILDING CLASSES
WHINING WORKS... BUT SQUIRM, AND BE PERSISTENT
MICHAEL FRY

"THE COSMOS IS ABOUT THE SMALLEST HOLE A MAN CAN HIDE HIS HEAD IN." -G.K. CHESTERTON-
YOU'RE NOT GETTING FAT... YOU'RE JUST FILLING THE VOID LEFT BY AN EXPANDING UNIVERSE.
MICHAEL FRY

BIG WHEEL
MY HARLEY'S IN THE SHOP...
IT'S OUR WAY OR THE DRIVEWAY!
TRIKER CHICKS
MICHAEL FRY

" I DO NOT LIKE GREEN EGGS AND HAM. I DO NOT LIKE THEM SAM-I-AM." -DR. SEUSS-

Nutrition Facts

Serving Size 2 Green Eggs and Ham
Servings per Container 1

Amount Per Serving	Mix	With a Fox In a Box
Calories	2000	2040
Calories from Fat	1999	2039
	% Daily Value*	
Total Fat 280g**	**300%**	**310%**
Saturated Fat 277g	**277%**	**303%**
Polyunsaturated Fat 1g	1%	3%
Monounsaturated Fat 1g	1%	3%
Cat in the Hat Fat 1g	1%	1%
Cholesterol 5043mg***	**1600%**	**1602%**
Green Dye #2 638mg	**8003%**	**8005%**
Fox 14h****	0%	3%

*Percent Daily Values are based on an 8000 calorie (pre-coronary) diet. Your daily values may be higher or lower depending on whether you're still breathing.
** Great Globs ***Massive Great Globs ****hairs

MICHAEL FRY

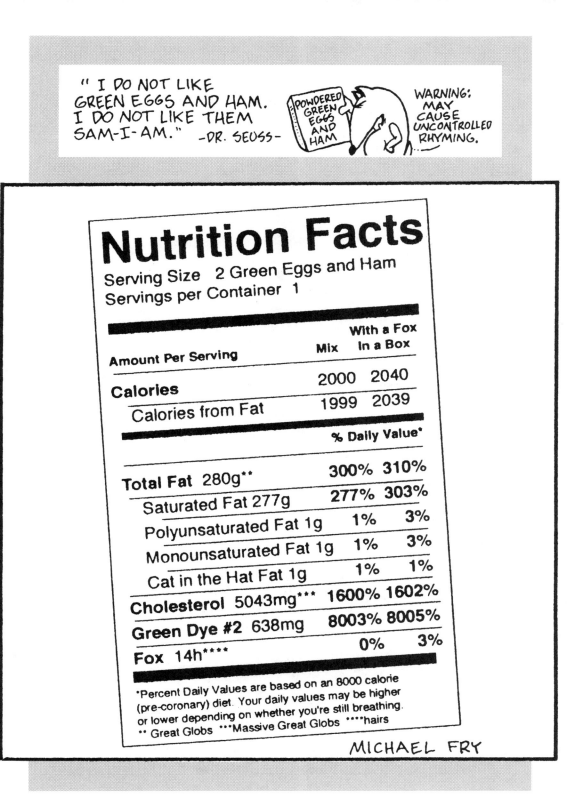

THE NEW PARENTING

SIT UP STRAIGHT.

DON'T TALK WITH YOUR MOUTH FULL. CHEW WITH YOUR MOUTH CLOSED.

DON'T TALK BACK. DON'T SAY "AIN'T." DON'T INTERRUPT.

DON'T RUN. DON'T JUMP. DON'T FALL. DON'T HURT YOURSELF.

FEET OFF THE FURNITURE. SHOES OFF THE STAIRS. CLOTHES OFF THE FLOOR.

SAY, "PLEASE." "THANK YOU." "EXCUSE ME." "MAY I." "HELLO." "GOODBYE." "GOOD NIGHT."

SMILE, DON'T SQUINT, DON'T PLAY WITH YOUR HAIR. PAY ATTENTION. DON'T WHINE. INSIDE VOICES, PLEASE.

PLAY QUIETLY.

THE **NEW** PART

...AND REMEMBER, YOU DON'T **HAVE** TO COLOR BETWEEN THE LINES.

MICHAEL FRY

HOW DID TRACY DO TODAY?

OH, FINE.

FINE?

FINE.

YOU KNOW, I'M AT WORK ALL DAY... AND I WONDER-

...WHAT'S SHE DOING NOW?... WHAT'S SHE THINKING? DID SHE EAT HER LUNCH? DID SHE FALL DOWN ON THE PLAYGROUND?

I'M JUST LOOKING FOR A FEW DETAILS!!

I JUST WANT A LITTLE REASSURANCE!

SHE'S FINE, REALLY...

SHE'S GOING TO TURN OUT JUST LIKE HER MOTHER...

AHHHHH

MICHAEL FRY

SOME THINGS YOU SWORE YOU'D NEVER SAY ONCE YOU BECAME A PARENT

"YES, I'LL HAVE ANOTHER TEETHING BISCUIT NACHO."

"WE DON'T LET OUR CHILD WATCH MR. ROGERS. WE FIND HIM VIOLENTLY NON-THREATENING"

CAN YOU SAY "PASSIVE-AGGRESSIVE"?

"AS PERFORMANCE ART, BARNEY ISN'T TOO BAD."

PURPLE HAZE, ALL IN MY MIND!

"NO, IT'S NOT AN EAR INFECTION; MY CHILD IS BEING ASSAULTED BACTERIALLY"

BABIES?... I THINK THEY COME FROM DETROIT.

...

"LINGUINE DOODLES MEET ALL MY CHILD'S NUTRITIONAL NEEDS."

LINGUINE DOODLES 88

"YOU DON'T HAVE TO COLOR BETWEEN THE LINES UNLESS, OF COURSE, YOU'RE BEING TESTED."

"ALL WE EXPECT IS FOR YOU TO DO YOUR BEST... AS LONG AS IT'S BETTER THAN EVERYONE ELSE."

MICHAEL FRY

WHAT WOMEN ARE THINKING

BELCH!

BELCH

MICHAEL FRY

PARENTS' LEAST FAVORITE WORDS

JOE! THERE YOU ARE!... I WANT YOU TO MEET MY COUSIN... HE'S A WRITER TOO!

JOE, THIS IS DERRICK MAUVE. HE WRITES FOR DISNEY!

WHOA!... SCREENWRITER...

JOE HERE IS A WRITER ALSO!

REALLY...

WELL, JUST FREE-LANCE... COPY-WRITING, SOME TECHNICAL STUFF, AIRLINE MAGS... HOW 'BOUT YOU? MAYBE I'VE SEEN YOUR STUFF.

DISNEYLAND?... SPACE MOUNTAIN?... THE SIGN ABOUT HALFWAY UP?

"FROM THIS POINT THE WAIT IS APPROXIMATELY 20 MINUTES."

I WROTE THAT.

WHO WAS THAT?

MY ILLUSION OF GRANDEUR.

MICHAEL FRY

HONEY, DO YOU THINK I'M FAT?

UH, OH...

...I COULD TELL THE TRUTH AND SAY THAT SHE NEVER DID LOSE THOSE COUPLE OF DOZEN POUNDS AFTER ZELDA WAS BORN.

...OR...

I COULD LIE AND SAY THAT SHE'S NEVER LOOKED BETTER. SHE SHOULD THINK OF THOSE EXTRA INCHES ON HER HIPS AS HAVING AN R-14 INSULATION FACTOR...

...OR...

...I COULD PRETEND I WAS KNOCKED OUT DURING A HOLD-UP AND COMPLETELY LOST MY MEMORY EXCEPT FOR A RECOLLECTION OF A PREVIOUS LIFE AS A STABLE BOY FOR A SPANISH CONQUISTADOR IN TIERRA DEL FUEGO.

WELL?

NO HABLO INGLES

MICHAEL FRY

WE WILL SERVE NO WHINE BEFORE ITS TIME.

PLEEEASE??
WHYYYY?
NOOOOOO!!

"FOOD IS AN IMPORTANT PART OF A BALANCED DIET."
-FRAN LEBOWITZ-

"THE GREATEST SERVICE WHICH CAN BE RENDERED ANY COUNTRY IS TO ADD A USEFUL PLANT TO ITS CULTURE."
-THOMAS JEFFERSON-

I DON'T DO PLANTS...
SNARF SNARF
BOB

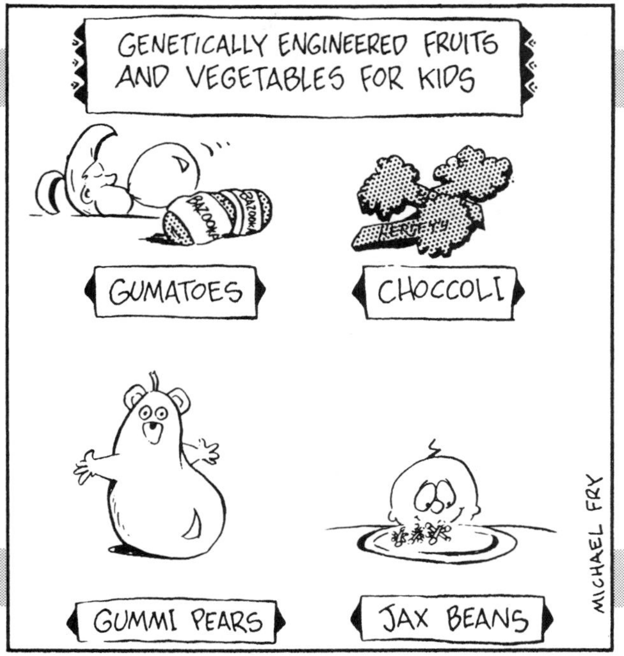

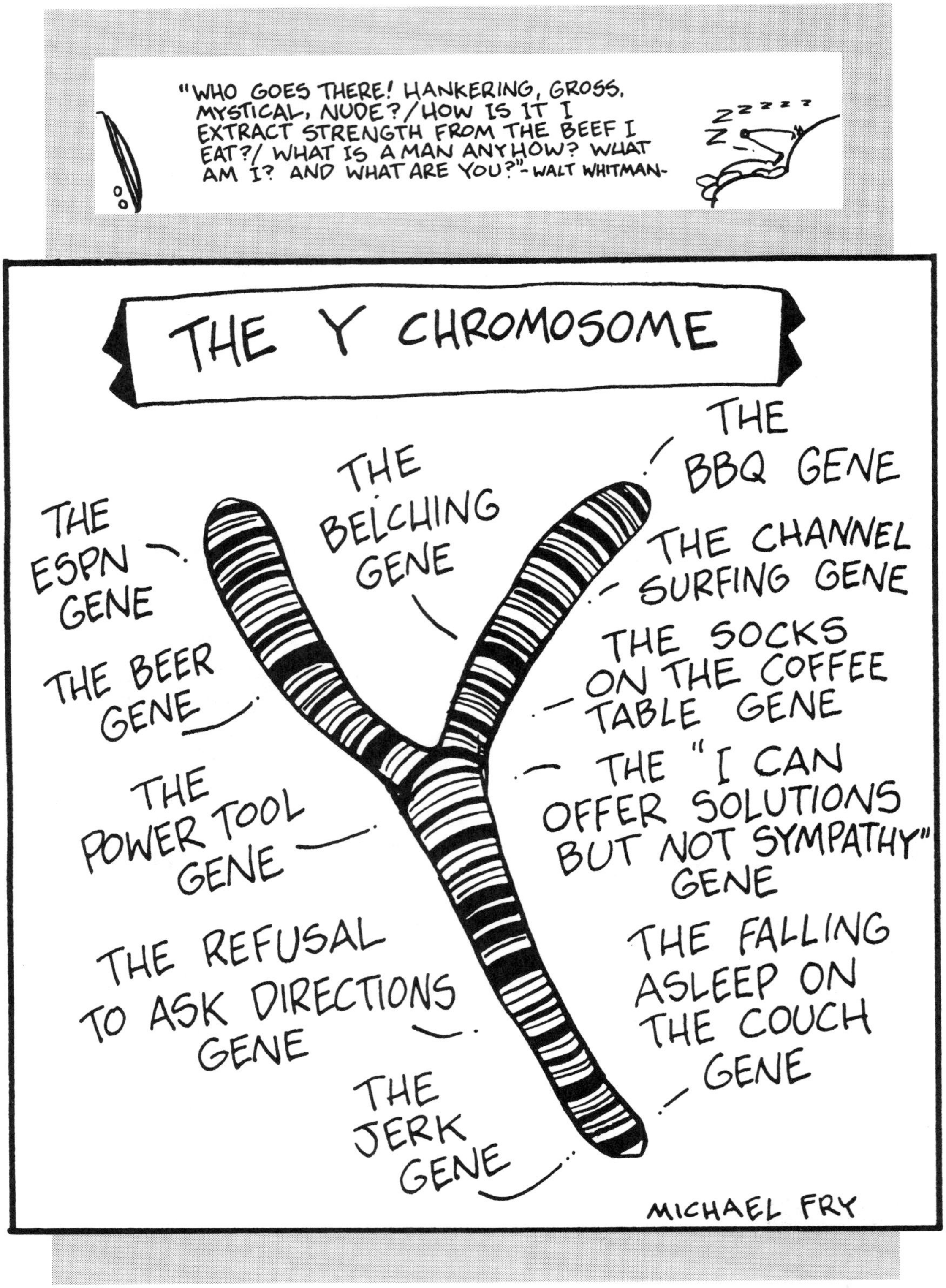

"WHO GOES THERE! HANKERING, GROSS, MYSTICAL, NUDE?/ HOW IS IT I EXTRACT STRENGTH FROM THE BEEF I EAT?/ WHAT IS A MAN ANYHOW? WHAT AM I? AND WHAT ARE YOU?" - WALT WHITMAN -

THE Y CHROMOSOME

THE ESPN GENE

THE BELCHING GENE

THE BBQ GENE

THE CHANNEL SURFING GENE

THE BEER GENE

THE SOCKS ON THE COFFEE TABLE GENE

THE "I CAN OFFER SOLUTIONS BUT NOT SYMPATHY" GENE

THE POWER TOOL GENE

THE REFUSAL TO ASK DIRECTIONS GENE

THE FALLING ASLEEP ON THE COUCH GENE

THE JERK GENE

MICHAEL FRY

WOMEN: COMPLEX EMOTIONAL CREATURES

I **WANT** HIM TO **SENSE** WHAT I WANT BEFORE I WANT IT AND WHAT I DON'T WANT BEFORE I DON'T WANT IT ANYMORE.

MEN: THIRSTY

I WANT A BEER.

MICHAEL FRY

I HATE WHEN THIS HAPPENS
BEDNOSE

From the creator of MORNING BREATH
comes a new level in horror...
BEDHEAD
You'll never look in the mirror again.
URP...
"No! No! Noooooo! AHHHHHHHHH!"
-Wes Craven-
" MOMMMMMMY"
-Stephen King-
MICHAEL FRY

WHICH TOOK LONGER TO BUILD?
THE PYRAMIDS....
..OR BARBIE'S FOLDING PALACE AT VERSAILLES?
INSERT TAPESTRY J OVER MIRROR T WHILE BEING CAREFUL NOT TO COVER CHERUB 48...
MICHAEL FRY

" SOME ASSEMBLY REQUIRED."
-ANONYMOUS-
HELP ME.

MOTHER GOOSE WAS A WORKING MOM

MOM!! NORMAN'S LOOKING AT ME!!

DID NOT! DID TOO! DID NOT! DID TOO!

JACK BE NIMBLE, JACK BE QUICK, JACK JUMP OVER A... AH... GUY NAMED RICK?... A BIG FAT TICK?... TRADER VIC?... NAH...

MOM!! GLENDA CALLED ME A TURKEY!!

DID NOT! DID TOO!!

MICHAEL FRY

IT'S HARDER THAN IT LOOKS!

"DO THIS... DON'T DO THAT... CAN'T YOU READ THE SIGNS."
- FIVE MAN ELECTRICAL BAND -
FEED ME

"VEGETABLES ARE INTERESTING BUT LACK A SENSE OF PURPOSE WHEN UNACCOMPANIED BY A GOOD CUT OF MEAT."
-FRAN LEBOWITZ-
I LIKE MY BEETS RARE, AS IN EXTINCT.
BEETS: IT'S WHAT'S FOR DINNER!!
BEETS
MICHAEL FRY

"TO CHILDREN CHILDHOOD HOLDS NO PARTICULAR ADVANTAGE."
-KATHLEEN NORRIS-
YOU'VE GOT IT MADE!
WHERE?!
NO NO NO NO NO NO NO NO NO NO NO NO NO NO NO NO NO NO NO NO NO NO NO NO NO NO NO NO
ARE YOU EVER GOING TO SAY YOUR FIRST WORD?
NO!
MICHAEL FRY

EEEEEEEEEEEEEEEEEEEEEEEEEEEEE
MY ESPRESSO MACHINE BLEW UP...
EEEEEEEEEEEEEE
SMOKE ALARM?!
BARBIE'S PLAYHOUSE SMOKE ALARM...
SHE LEFT THE CURLING IRON IN TOO LONG.
EEEEEEEEEEEEEEEEEEEE
MICHAEL FRY

"LIFE IS TOO SHORT TO STUFF A MUSHROOM."
-SHIRLEY CONRAN-
YOU DON'T TAKE PLASTIC? HOW 'BOUT VINYL? POLY-STYRENE? BUBBLE-WRAP?
THE COMPLETE 15-MINUTE MEAL AS IT APPEARS IN THE MAGAZINE
AND AS IT APPEARS IN YOUR HOME
MICHAEL FRY

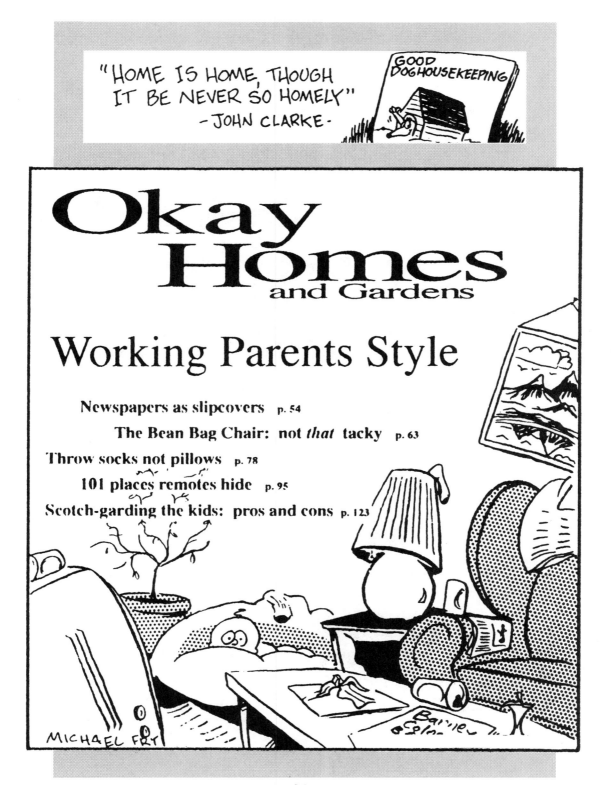

"HOME IS HOME, THOUGH IT BE NEVER SO HOMELY"
-JOHN CLARKE-

GOOD DOGHOUSEKEEPING

MONSTER WAGON
HELP!
OOF!

THE MONSTER TRIKE RALLY
I CAN'T REACH THE PEDALS.
MICHAEL FRY

HOW TO EAT SPAGHETTI
GRASP
SMUCK
TWIRL
WEEEEEEE
STRETCH
SQUEAK SQUEAK SQUEAK SQUEAK
INHALE
SLURP
MICHAEL FRY

"EVERYTHING YOU SEE I OWE TO SPAGHETTI."
-SOPHIA LOREN-
SLURP
LOOK, NO HANDS!

ARE WE THERE YET? I HAVE TO GO TO THE BATHROOM. WA
SHE'S TOUCHING ME! ARE WE THERE YET? I HAVE TO GO TO
BATHROOM. WAAAAAAAA!!! SHE'S TOUCHING ME! ARE WE

QUANTITY TIME

HELP!!!

MICHAEL FRY

AREN'T YOU GLAD YOU HAVE CHILDREN?...

DON'T YOU WISH EVERYONE DID?

" IF THERE WERE NO SCHOOLS TO TAKE THE CHILDREN AWAY FROM HOME... ... THE INSANE ASYLUM WOULD BE FILLED WITH MOTHERS."

-EDGAR WATSON HOWE-

THERE WAS AN OLD WOMAN WHO LIVED IN A SHOE, SHE HAD SO MANY CHILDREN SHE DIDN'T KNOW WHAT TO DO.

HOW MANY CHILDREN DID SHE HAVE?

TWO.

MICHAEL FRY

"QUIT WORRYING ABOUT YOUR HEALTH. IT'LL GO AWAY."
-ROBERT ORBEN-
Z.
GREAT MOMENTS IN INTERIOR DESIGN
THE POST-MODERN OTTOMAN
EXERFLEX
MICHAEL FRY

YOU KNOW, IF I SQUINT REAL HARD I LOOK LIKE LASSIE BEFORE THE NOSE JOB.
OH, IS THIS A PICTURE OF YOUR KIDS?
HOW OLD IS THE BIG ONE?
35.
MICHAEL FRY

"HE'S A WICKED MAN THAT COMES AFTER CHILDREN WHEN THEY WON'T GO TO BED AND THROWS HANDFULS OF SAND IN THEIR EYES." -ERNST HOFFMAN-
ALL I HAVE TO DO IS CLOSE MY EYES AND I-
ZZZ ZZZ ZZZ
IS SHE ASLEEP YET?
NOT YET.
MICHAEL FRY

WAAAAAA!!!
IF SHE DIDN'T WANT HER FACE LICKED, THEN SHE SHOULDN'T HAVE SMEARED PEANUT BUTTER ALL OVER IT...
LOOK AT YOUR FACE!
LICK
RUB RUB RUB
MGMPHLX...
11/23
SPIT: THE UNIVERSAL SOLVENT
EEEUUUUUUUU
DRIP
DRIP
MICHAEL FRY

ALAS, POOR FROSTY, I KNEW HIM WELL.
DRIP DRIP DRIP

SNOWMAN-O-RAMA
12 ANGRY SNOWMEN
THE SNOWMAN OF LA MANCHA
OF MICE AND SNOWMEN
A SNOWMAN FOR ALL SEASONS
MICHAEL FRY

SANTA'S LITTLE HELPERS
GRUMPY
HEY! DO I LOOK LIKE A JOLLY OLD ELF?! TAKE IT UP WITH THE FAT GUY!
SANTA WILL RETURN:
GIDDY
YOU WANT TO GROW UP AND BE AN ELF? DRINK LOTS OF COFFEE! STUNTS YOUR GROWTH!
YEAH!
SANTA WILL RETURN
SNOOTY
AND YOU ARE?... AND YOU'RE WITH?...
SANTA WILL RETURN
MICHAEL FRY
DAMIEN
PULL HIS BEARD... CALL HIM JELL-O GUT... HE LOVES THAT!
SANTA LEFT

I WOULD LIKE PEACE ON EARTH, GOODWILL TOWARD DOGS, AND A REALLY EFFECTIVE FLEA SHAMPOO.

"GUILT IS A ROPE THAT WEARS THIN."

-AYN RAND-

DOGS NEVER FEEL GUILTY...

...SINCE WE CAN'T REMEMBER THE DAY BEFORE YESTERDAY.

"NEVER ALLOW YOUR CHILD TO CALL YOU BY YOUR FIRST NAME. HE HASN'T KNOWN YOU LONG ENOUGH."

-FRAN LEBOWITZ-

BOB!

MR. "THE DOG" TO YOU...

BUT I WANT TO GO TO SCHOOL NAKED!
EXCUSE ME?... IS THAT ANY WAY TO ASK?
PLEEEEEEEEEEEEASE CAN I GO TO SCHOOL NAKED?
THAT'S BETTER... NOW,...
...ARE YOU OUT OF YOUR MIND?
ZING
ZING
MICHAEL FRY

"HE THAT BRINGETH A PRESENT FINDETH THE DOOR OPEN."
-THOMAS FULLER-
FOR SANTA
MILK & COOKIES AND A TEN SPOT
IT'S NOT A BRIBE, IT'S A TIP!
BARBIE IS A HARMLESS, MISUNDERSTOOD, POLITICALLY INCORRECT PRISONER OF WAR!... DO THE RIGHT THING... SET BARBIE FREE!!
DON'T BRIBE THE SANTA, DEAR...
CHA-CHING
CHA-CHING
MICHAEL FRY

IF YOU ASK ME, WASHING YOUR FOOD BEFORE YOU EAT IT IS A COMPLETE WASTE OF TIME...
SCRUB
SCRUB
DOG FOOD
DOG FOOD
SCRUB SCRUB SCRUB
NO, I DON'T THINK THERE'S ANY PESTICIDE RESIDUE LEFT.
MICHAEL FRY

BOB THE RED-NOSED REINDOG
G.E. HALOGEN RED NOSE
RED-NOSED REINDEER SUPPORT GROUP
THEY WOULDN'T LET ME PLAY ANY REINDEER GAMES!
EXCEPT, "RED LIGHT, GREEN LIGHT."
WHY CAN'T IT BE FOGGY EVERY CHRISTMAS?
NOW, A BLACK LIGHT NOSE!...THAT'D BE BOSS!
MICHAEL FRY

THAT'S SOME COLEMAN LANTERN THEY GOT.
THERE WAS NO ROOM AT THE INN SO THEY DECIDED TO GO CAMPING.
MICHAEL FRY

" IF ONE IS LUCKY, A SOLITARY FANTASY CAN TOTALLY TRANSFORM A THOUSAND REALITIES."

—MAYA ANGELOU

WORKING MOM FANTASY #2

YOU TRADED IN THE MINI-VAN?!!

MICHAEL FRY

HEY, MOM! DID YOU KNOW THAT BARBIE IS 35 YEARS OLD THIS YEAR? THAT'S THE SAME AGE AS YOU!
HMM...
GRRRRR
TWIST
POP!
AHHHH
MICHAEL FRY
HAPPY BIRTHDAY...

THE DUST MITE CONVENTION
WELCOME MITES
SAM?
FRANK?
I HAVEN'T SEEN YOU IN YEARS!
DITTO, OLD BOY! WHERE ARE YOU BURROWING THESE DAYS?
LUCY AND I AND THE SIX MILLION KIDDOS ARE SETTLED IN THE LA-Z-BOY
SIX?! WE'VE ONLY GOT TWO! YOU'RE IN THE 'BURBS, HUH?
IT'S COMFORTABLE, SECURE AND DUST AS FAR AS THE EYE CAN SEE... HOW 'BOUT YOU?
WE'VE GOT A CONDO IN THE VACUUM CLEANER.
WELCOME MITES TO THE PILLOW ROOM
YOU DOG! LIVIN' THE HIGH LIFE!
IT DOESN'T GET ANY DUSTIER THAN THAT!
PARRRTY!!
DID YOU SAY SOMETHING?
MICHAEL FRY

YOU WANT **WHAT** FOR CHRISTMAS?

BARBIE AND HER BIKINI PLAY SET!

LET'S TALK

YOU SEE BARBIE'S FEET? THEY'RE FUSED IN THE HIGH-HEEL POSITION.

SO?

LET'S TRY LOOKING IN THIS CATALOG.

P.C. TOYS Я US

OH, LOOK! "NATURE-FEM." SHE'S WEARING A NON-BLEACHED COTTON DRESS AND TEENY TINY BIRKENSTOCK SANDALS.

HER HAIR ISN'T PERMED...

HER EYEBROWS HAVE GROWN TOGETHER

YOU'RE NOT HELPING ME!!

$129.95?! FORGET IT!

SHE'S MADE ENTIRELY FROM RECYCLED EVIAN BOTTLES!

WHERE'S HER THONG BIKINI?

MICHAEL FRY

WHAT YOU WANT FOR CHRISTMAS

CHOCOLA SYRUP

MY-SIZE PRINCESS OF ALL SHE SURVEYS

WIDE SCREEN

ISLAND AIRWAYS TICKET

ISLA AIRWA TICKE

WHAT YOU'LL GET FOR CHRISTMAS

THE IMAGINATION BLOCKS

THEY'RE WOOD! THEY'RE SQUARE! THEY STACK!

MY-SIZE POST-FEMINIST WOMAN OF INDEPENDENT MEANS

TV GUIDE

TIKI TORCHES

HAWAII NOT INCLUDED

MICHAEL FRY

12:01 A.M. JANUARY 1, 1960

Z.

12:01 A.M. JANUARY 1, 1968

JOIN JOHNNY AND HIS GUESTS, ROBERT GOULET, JOEY BISHOP AND THAT GUY WHO DOES THAT TWIRLING THING WITH THE DISHES.

12:01 A.M. JANUARY 1, 1978

YEAH... TIMES SQUARE... GOOD IDEA... YEAH...

12:01 A.M. JANUARY 1, 1984

12:01 A.M. JANUARY 1, 1988

PUNT!

BOBBLE BOBBLE

BOBBLE BOBBLE

12:01 A.M. JANUARY 1, 1995

Z. Z.

MICHAEL FRY

I LOVE YOU DADDY.

I LOVE YOU TOO, SWEETHEART.

BUT I LOVE YOU BEST, RAGGEDY ANDY...

OUR DAUGHTER JUST EXPRESSED HER PREFERENCE FOR AN INANIMATE OBJECT THAT JUST LAYS AROUND AND DOES NOTHING!

I LOVE YOU TOO, DEAR...

MICHAEL FRY

NO, YOU CAN'T HAVE ANOTHER TREAT, IT'S TOO CLOSE TO SUPPERTIME.

DO YOU REALIZE OUR ROLE AS PARENTS IS BASICALLY ADVERSARIAL?

WE HAVE TO BE THE BAD GUYS. WE HAVE TO SAY NO. WE HAVE TO PROTECT THEM FROM THEIR WORST IMPULSES.

I DON'T KNOW... I GUESS I THOUGHT IT WAS GOING TO BE MORE FUN.

DON'T WORRY, IT'LL BE FUN SOMEDAY.

WHEN?

MOM?... DAD?... CAN WE DRESS BOB UP LIKE MARY POPPINS AND THROW HIM OFF THE ROOF TO SEE IF HE'LL FLY?

OHMYGOD OHMYGOD OHMYGOD OHMYGOD

NO.

NO.

MICHAEL FRY

WE NEVER GET TO HAVE ANY FUN!

...THE FUN STARTS WHEN **THEY** HAVE CHILDREN!

THANKYOU THANKYOU

THANKYOU THANKYOU

WHAT WOULD YOU RECOMMEND BETWEEN THE...

...HEART ATTACK ON A PLATE,

...THE TRANS-FATTY ACIDS WITH A HORMONE CHUTNEY, OR THE...

...LIGHTLY GRILLED E. COLI WITH AN ANTIBIOTIC GLAZE?

WELL SIR, THE HEART ATTACK IS OUR SPECIALTY.

GOOD ENOUGH FOR ME!

MICHAEL FRY

WOULD YOU LIKE THAT WITH **EXTRA** LOW-DENSITY LIPO-PROTEINS?

YOU BET!

SATURDAY NIGHT AT "CHEZ C'EST LA VIE"

AND FOR YOU, MA'AM?

JUST A SALAD.

PESTICIDE RESIDUE OR GENETICALLY ALTERED?...

ALTERED. I'M ON A DIET.

"STUDIES SHOW THAT WHILE WOMEN UNREALISTICALLY DISTORT THEIR BODIES NEGATIVELY, MEN UNREALISTICALLY DISTORT THEIRS POSITIVELY."

—NAOMI WOLF—

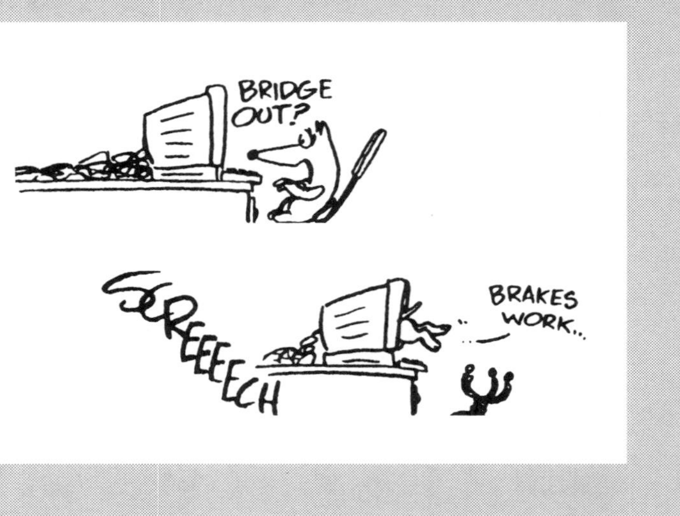

"IT'S NOT ENOUGH TO HAVE A GOOD MIND. THE MAIN THING IS TO USE IT WELL."

—RENE DESCARTES—

I'M BURNED OUT AGAIN...

"I'M NOT DENYIN' THE WOMEN ARE FOOLISH. GOD ALMIGHTY MADE 'EM TO MATCH THE MEN."
—GEORGE ELIOT—

THE X CHROMOSOME

THE "I'LL HAVE A PIECE OF DOUBLE CHOCOLATE CHEESE-CAKE WITH A DIET COKE" GENE.

THE "WHY CAN'T YOU ASK DIRECTIONS" GENE

THE "WE COULD EAT OFF THIS FLOOR" GENE

THE "I LOVED BARBIE AS A CHILD" GENE

THE "WHY CAN'T MY HUSBAND'S TUSH LOOK LIKE MEL GIBSON'S TUSH" GENE

THE "I HATE BARBIE AS AN ADULT" GENE

THE "DON'T GET READY TO GO OUT UNTIL FIVE MINUTES BEFORE YOU'RE SUPPOSED TO BE THERE" GENE.

THE "I MAY NOT KNOW WHAT I WANT, BUT I KNOW I DON'T WANT IT FROM YOU" GENE

THE "MY KID WILL GROW UP TO BE A FELON IF I DON'T STAY UP ALL NIGHT FOR A WEEK MAKING HER HALLOWEEN COSTUME" GENE

MICHAEL FRY

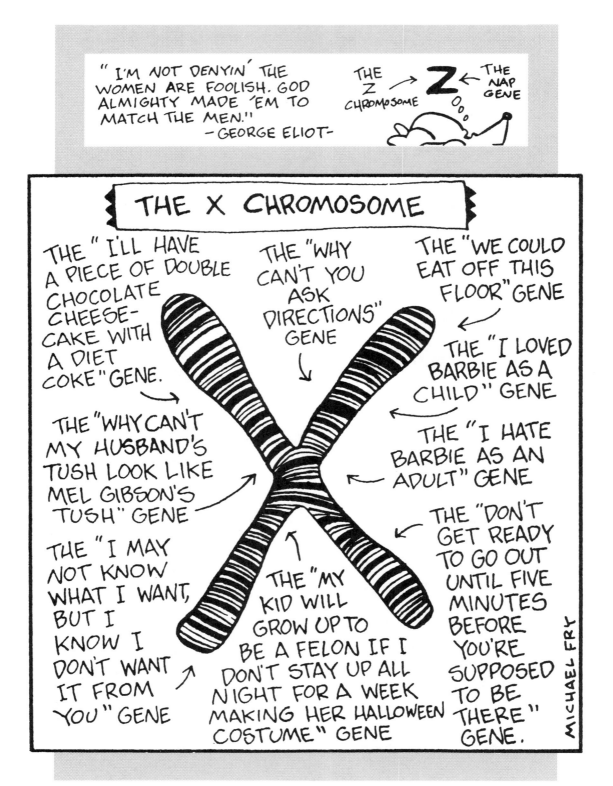

"YOU KNOW, I HATE FIGHTING. IF I KNEW HOW TO MAKE A LIVING SOME OTHER WAY, I WOULD."
-MUHAMMAD ALI-
HIS BARK IS WORSE THAN HIS BITE.
DOGGIE DENTURES
ACTION FIGURE SUPPORT GROUPS
HI, MY NAME IS JOE AND ALL I EVER WANTED TO BE WAS A FLORIST.
HI JOE!!!
G.I. JOE
MICHAEL FRY

YOU'RE NOT REAL... I DON'T BELIEVE YOU EXIST... YOU'RE A FIGMENT OF MY IMAGINATION AND I'LL GET YOU A RIB-EYE, LICKETY SPLIT!
THE PETERSON GUIDE TO COMMON NORTH AMERICAN MONSTERS
HE'S GOT GREEN JELLY WARTS, HORNS AND BREATH AS BAD AS AUNT DOREEN'S.
HMM... COULD BE A SPECKLED, PAINT-PEELING BEDBEAST... DOES HE OOZE YELLOW SLIME?
MICHAEL FRY

I WAS DEPRESSED ABOUT THE LACK OF DIRECTION IN MY LIFE.
SO THE VET PUT ME ON ANTI-DEPRESSANTS.
IT WORKED! I'VE COMPLETELY STOPPED CHASING MY TAIL!
EAR PLUGS?
PROZAC.
WAAAAAAA
MICHAEL FRY

MUCK MUCK
STAIN PERSISTENT
THERE'S ONLY ONE WAY TO HANDLE THOSE REALLY TOUGH STAINS
MICHAEL FRY
GAS
WHOOSH!

"HIS SLEEP WAS A SENSUOUS GLUTTONY OF OBLIVION."
-P.D. JAMES-
A GLUT OF OBLIVION

BY THREE MONTHS, 70% OF INFANTS ARE SLEEPING FROM MIDNIGHT TO 5 A.M.
BY ONE YEAR, 90% DO.
AND 10% DON'T.
AND .001% THINK IT'S FUNNY
MICHAEL FRY

Good Enough Housekeeping
How Much Dirt...
...Can You Sweep Under a Carpet?
101 Macaroni & Cheese Mix-Ins
Froot Loops...Spam...Yogurt Raisins
Strip Mining Sofas
"There's change in them thar cushions"
MICHAEL FRY

" AT THE WORST A HOUSE UNKEPT CANNOT BE SO DISTRESSING AS A LIFE UNLIVED."
-ROSE MACAULAY-
WHEN MY HOUSE GETS DIRTY I JUST MOVE.
BOB

THE CHILDREN'S DICTIONARY

treat *n* / trēt/ a right, an entitlement, an expectation upon completion of a ridiculously easy task, a crucial part of an unbalanced diet, the holy grail, the source of all happiness, that which gives life meaning. *syn:* **sugar**. *ant:* **sugar-free.**

Whatever it was on their dessert plates, Tracy and Zelda felt sure it wasn't a **treat**.

MONGREL n/mun' grəl/ THE KING OF DOGS, GENETICALLY SUPERIOR, SUPERPOOCH

I SWEAR THAT'S WHAT IT SAYS!

WARNING: SLEEPS, EATS, SCRATCHES... MAY SPONTANEOUSLY YAWN. NOT RESPONSIBLE FOR MUCH OF ANYTHING.

WHAT YOU SEE IS WHAT YOU PET.

WARNING: Handle with care. Keep upright. Do not shake. Contents under pressure. Keep in warm dry place. Not responsible for spills, leaks or sudden eruptions. May smell, yell, cry, whine, annoy, disappoint, excite and cause extreme happiness. Laughter may be contagious. Do not operate heavy machinery while under its influence. Warranty void if not hugged. Love at your own risk.

"PARENTS LEARN A LOT FROM THEIR CHILDREN ABOUT COPING WITH LIFE." -MURIEL SPARK-
WAAAAA
IT'S 3 A.M. DO YOU KNOW WHERE YOUR CHILD IS?
WAAAA
YES.
MICHAEL FRY

CRUNCH!... OW!... I'M OKAY!
SMASH... GROAN!... STILL HERE!
SPLAT!... MOAN!... NEVER BETTER!
WALK IT OFF.
CARTOON FOCUS GROUPS
DO YOU FEEL VERY STRONGLY, SOMEWHAT STRONGLY, NOT TOO STRONGLY, OR NOT AT ALL THAT AN ANVIL IS THE FUNNIEST WAY TO CRUSH WILE E. COYOTE INTO AN ACCORDION.
MICHAEL FRY

"TO MULTIPLY THE HARBORS DOES NOT REDUCE THE SEA." -EMILY DICKINSON-
IN CASE BOB HAS AN ACTION-ADVENTURE DREAM
REALLY REALLY SLOW
PARENTS PANICKING
RADAR ENFORCED
HANG ON... HERE COMES ANOTHER SPEED BUMP!
WEEEEEE.
AIR BAG
ANTI-LOCK BRAKES
RADIO FLYER
MICHAEL FRY

BOB HERE IS FIVE. THAT'S THIRTY-FIVE TO YOU AND ME.
OHMYGOD... YUCK! I'M A BABY BOOMER!
BIRTHDAY PARTIES OF THE FUN-IMPAIRED
YOU FILLED THE PINATA WITH...
...YOGURT FOR EVERYBODY!
GLOP
MICHAEL FRY

"BRAIN, n. AN APPARATUS WITH WHICH WE THINK THAT WE THINK."

-AMBROSE BIERCE-

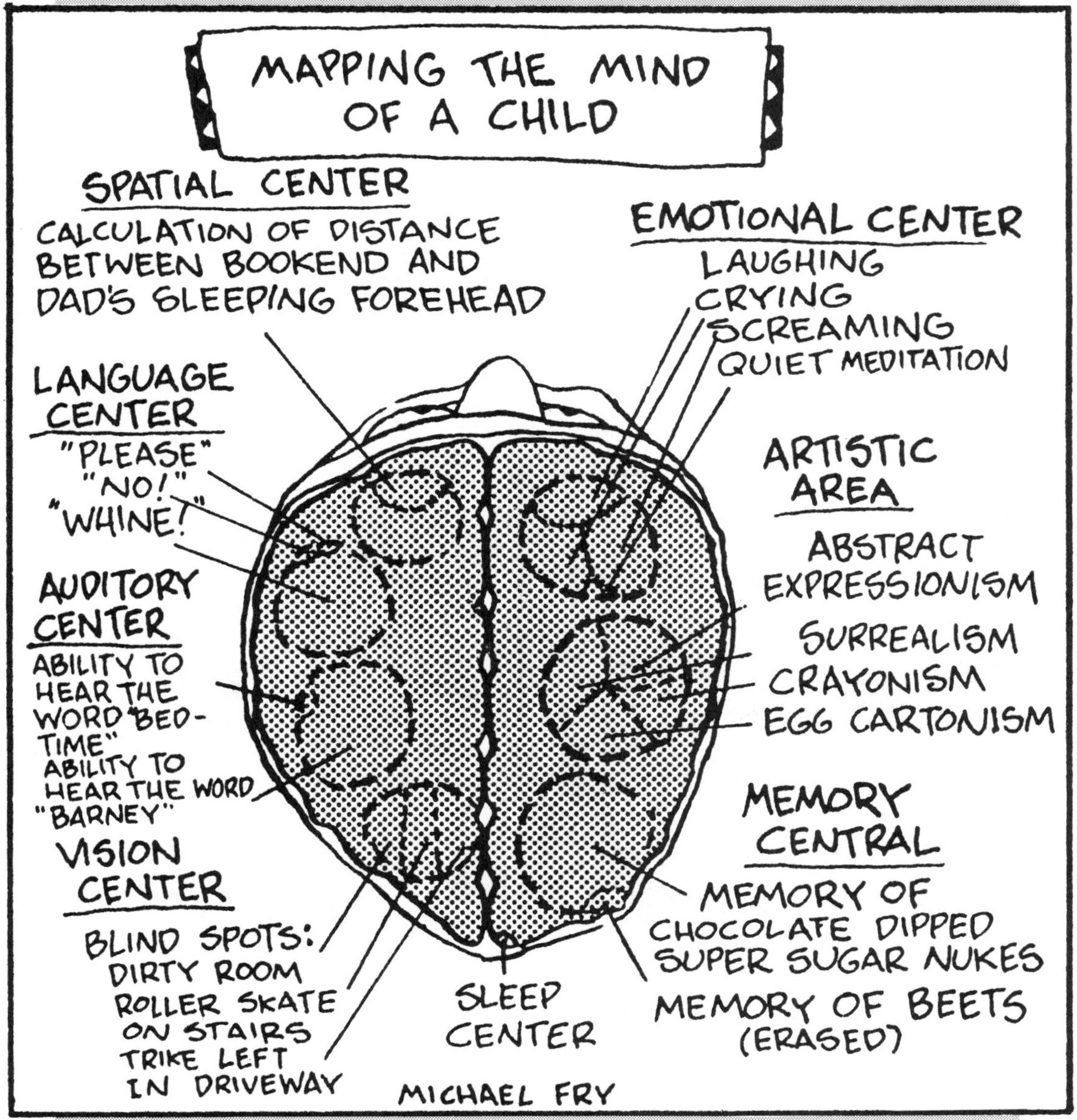

MAPPING THE MIND OF A CHILD

SPATIAL CENTER
CALCULATION OF DISTANCE BETWEEN BOOKEND AND DAD'S SLEEPING FOREHEAD

EMOTIONAL CENTER
LAUGHING
CRYING
SCREAMING
QUIET MEDITATION

LANGUAGE CENTER
"PLEASE"
"NO!"
"WHINE!"

ARTISTIC AREA
ABSTRACT EXPRESSIONISM
SURREALISM
CRAYONISM
EGG CARTONISM

AUDITORY CENTER
ABILITY TO HEAR THE WORD "BED-TIME"
ABILITY TO HEAR THE WORD "BARNEY"

MEMORY CENTRAL
MEMORY OF CHOCOLATE DIPPED SUPER SUGAR NUKES
MEMORY OF BEETS (ERASED)

VISION CENTER
BLIND SPOTS:
DIRTY ROOM
ROLLER SKATE ON STAIRS
TRIKE LEFT IN DRIVEWAY

SLEEP CENTER

MICHAEL FRY

"YOU HAVE TO LOVE YOUR CHILDREN UNSELFISHLY. THAT'S HARD. BUT IT'S THE ONLY WAY."

-BARBARA BUSH-

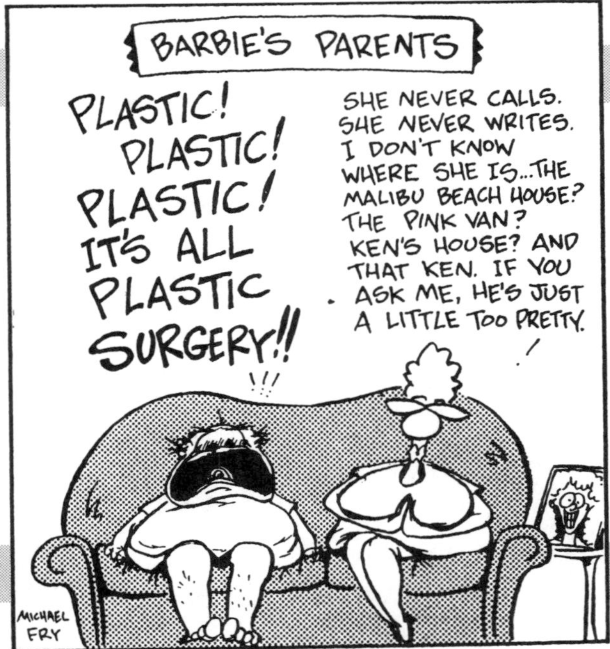

Whenever you see this seal you'll know that what you're buying is good enough. It'll be unpretentious, not extravagant and will be available in two colors: avocado and beige. It will have three speeds: slow, fast, and not too fast. It will work well but not too well. Nothing lasts forever and neither will this. But that's what you expect. And we guarantee nothing less.

MICHAEL FRY

"MEDIOCRITY IS SAFE."

-NIKKI GIOVANNI-

GOOD ENOUGH DOG

COULD BE WORSE

YOU'RE LUCKY TO HAVE HIM

NOT TOO BAD

TOTAL QUALITY FAMILY MANAGEMENT
WE ARE NOT REACHING OUR GOAL THIS QUARTER OF A 50% IMPROVEMENT IN MATERNAL SATISFACTION.
MICHAEL FRY

BOB'S GREATEST FEAR
DOWNSIZING!
AYEEEE!!

"THE LORD PREFERS COMMON LOOKING PEOPLE. THAT'S WHY HE MADE SO MANY OF THEM."
-ABRAHAM LINCOLN-
COMMON DOG

WHAT DO YOU THINK, HONEY? BOXERS?
OR BRIEFS?
PANTS.
MICHAEL FRY

"IT DOESN'T MUCH SIGNIFY WHOM ONE MARRIES, FOR ONE IS SURE TO FIND NEXT MORNING IT WAS SOMEONE ELSE."

-SAMUEL ROGERS-

WANT TO SPICE UP THAT MARRIAGE? TRY A LITTLE FANTASY...

I'M PICTURING MEL GIBSON IN A SATIN ROBE CARRYING A BOTTLE OF CHAMPAGNE AND A SINGLE FIVE-INCH STILETTO GLASS SLIPPER.

MICHAEL FRY

JUST REMEMBER **NOT** TO OPEN YOUR EYES

?

BRUSH BRUSH

AHHHHHHH!!!!!!

SCRATCH SCRATCH

"AND WHAT IS WRONG IN WOMEN'S LIFE IN MAN'S CANNOT BE RIGHT."
-FRANCES ELLEN WATKINS HAPER-
I HAD IT ALL, THEN I LOST IT.
I FORGOT WHERE I BURIED IT.
THE PROBLEM WOMEN FACE
HOW CAN I HAVE A SATISFYING MARRIAGE, RAISE SUCCESSFUL KIDS AND DEVELOP A FULFILLING CAREER ALL AT THE SAME TIME?
SIMPLE. I'LL HELP...
THE FACE OF THEIR PROBLEM
...RIGHT AFTER "THE X FILES."
MICHAEL FRY

"EAST, WEST. HOME'S BEST."
-PROVERB-
YES, I'M INTO HOME IMPROVEMENT... I WATCH IT EVERY WEEK!
BOB
EARLY HOME IMPROVEMENT
GROAN! WE NEVER HAD A DOOR WHEN I WAS GROWING UP! OOF!
GIVE ME A BREAK, YOU WERE A TREE DWELLER!
CAVE DEPOT
YOU CAN DO IT YOURSELF
DOORS
BIG
MICHAEL FRY

THE "PROPER" WAY TO PICK A DOG
OH, YEAH... NOW THIS IS COMFORTABLE
THE PROPER WAY TO PICK UP A CHILD
WRONG
RIGHT
LIFT WITH THE LEGS
MICHAEL FRY

BOB'S LIST OF CHORES
1. BURY REMOTE
2. BARK AT MAILMAN
3. CHASE TAIL
4. REPEAT
I NEED TO REDUCE THE STRESS IN MY LIFE
OKAY, I'LL WRITE DOWN ALL THE HOUSEHOLD CHORES I DO AND YOU WRITE DOWN ALL THE CHORES YOU DO.
IS "LOVE SLAVE" TWO WORDS OR HYPHENATED?
MICHAEL FRY

I JUST LOVE MY FLOPSY, MOPSY, COTTON-TAIL AND PETER RABBIT COMMEMORATIVE CHEW TOYS!

PETER RABBIT, MR. McGREGOR AND THEIR ATTORNEY ON RICKI LAKE
ALL THE BOOKS, THE DOLLS, THE CHINA, THE LOOT! WE GOT NONE OF THAT! ZILCH! I'VE GOT 700 MOUTHS TO FEED!
IT'S NOT ABOUT MONEY, IT'S ABOUT RESPECT! WE WANT FIVE MILLION DOLLARS WORTH OF RESPECT!
MICHAEL FRY

IF KIDS WERE DESIGNED WITH PARENTS IN MIND
View
Label
Special
Clean up Window
Empty Trash
Eject Disk
Erase Disk
Restart
Shut Down
Sleep
MICHAEL FRY

IF DOGS WERE DESIGNED WITH OWNERS IN MIND
HEY! RELAX! I'LL WALK MYSELF!

7 p.m

(11) **Onesomething** (debut) From the producers of "thirtysomething" comes this exploration of toddler angst. Tonight, Michael screams, Nancy spits up, Hope yawns and Elliot is dropped on his head. * * *

" TELEVISION HAS PROVED THAT PEOPLE WILL LOOK AT ANYTHING RATHER THAN EACH OTHER."

- ANN LANDERS -

eye Rib-eye Rib-eye Rib-
Rib-eye Rib-eye Rib-eye Rib-eye
Rib-eye Rib-eye Rib-eye Rib-eye
h-eye Rib-eye Rib-eye Rib

WHAT PARENTS ARE THINKING

P SLEEP SLEEP SLEEP SLEEP SLEEP
S SLEEP KIDS SLEEP SLEEP SLEEP SL
OD SLEEP WORK SLEEP SLEEP SLEEP S
LEEP SLEEP SLEEP SLEEP KIDS SLEEP SL
SLEEP SLEEP SLEEP SLEEP KIDS SLEEP SL
SLEEP SLEEP SLEEP SLEEP SLEEP SLEEP S
SLEEP KIDS SLEEP SLEEP SLEEP SLEEP SL
LEEP SLEEP SLEEP SLEEP SLEEP SLEEP
EEP SLEEP SLEEP SLEEP SLEEP SLEE
P SLEEP SLEEP SLEEP SLEEP SLE
EEP SLEEP SLEEP SLEEP SL

MICHAEL FRY

YOU KNOW HOW WHEN YOU LEAVE AND THEN YOU COME BACK FIVE MINUTES LATER AND WE DOGS BEHAVE LIKE WE HAVEN'T SEEN YOU FOR THIRTY YEARS?...
IT'S AN ACT... IT'S JUST A PUBLIC SERVICE TO MAKE YOU FEEL WANTED... HONEST!
DAY CARE DROP-OFF
DON'T LEAVE ME! DON'T LEAVE ME! DON'T LEAVE ME! DON'T LEAVE ME!
FIVE SECONDS AFTER YOU LEAVE
I'M COOL... I JUST LIKE TO MESS WITH HER MIND.
MICHAEL FRY

"WE ARE UNDER-EXERCISED AS A NATION. WE LOOK INSTEAD OF PLAY. WE RIDE INSTEAD OF WALK." -JOHN F. KENNEDY-
NO-IMPACT AEROBICS
Z.
THE SEDENTARY BICYCLE
HONEY? CAN YOU GET ME ANOTHER BEER?!
MICHAEL FRY

Legos
Z.
MICHAEL FRY
Legos
Legos
IF I'VE TOLD YOU ONCE, I'VE TOLD YOU A MILLION TIMES... STOP ENTOMBING YOUR FATHER!
HELP!

"THERE ARE MEN I COULD SPEND AN ETERNITY WITH, BUT NOT IN THIS LIFE." -KATHLEEN NORRIS-
SPEND ETERNITY WITH BOB
IT'LL BE OVER WITH BEFORE YOU KNOW IT!
MARRIAGE
WITH SUBTITLES
THANKS FOR YOUR HELP *
NO BOTHER **
* Who is this person? He's not my husband. My husband would be watching, "Bowling for Donuts."
** It's a rerun.
MICHAEL FRY

"THE BEST THINGS IN LIFE ARE FREE."
BUDDY DE SYLVA

WHAT YOU DID WITH ALL THAT FREE TIME BEFORE YOU HAD KIDS.

Z.

Z.

MICHAEL FRY

THE FIVE KINDS OF INTELLIGENCE

SPATIAL

$$\frac{\text{VASE}}{\sqrt{23}\,(64x)b}\left(\frac{c^2}{\frac{d}{\text{FOREHEAD}}}\right) = \text{PAIN}$$

Z.

MATHEMATICAL

HOW MANY COOKIES DID YOU EAT ?!

MGHMPH... 63... URP!

PHYSICAL

WEEEEEEEE...

A TRIPLE!

WITHOUT A NET!!

VERBAL

AHHH

TRANSLATION?

"I WET, THEREFORE I CHAFE."

SCREAM ENGLISH

ARTISTIC

YOU TOLD HER SHE DIDN'T HAVE TO COLOR BETWEEN THE LINES.

MICHAEL FRY

RING RING

HELLO... OH, HI, MOM. SORRY I HAVEN'T CALLED. I'VE BEEN BUSY.

..SORRY... ...SORRY... ...SORRY... ...SORRY...

...I'LL TRY HARDER, MOM...

'BYE, MOM. TAKE CARE OF YOURSELF

CLICK

I'M SORRY I'M SUCH A BIG DISAPPOINTMENT TO YOU!!

YOUR MOM?

SHE'S SICK AGAIN.

OH,... THAT PESKY COLD?

NO... POST-PARTUM DEPRESSION.

MICHAEL FRY

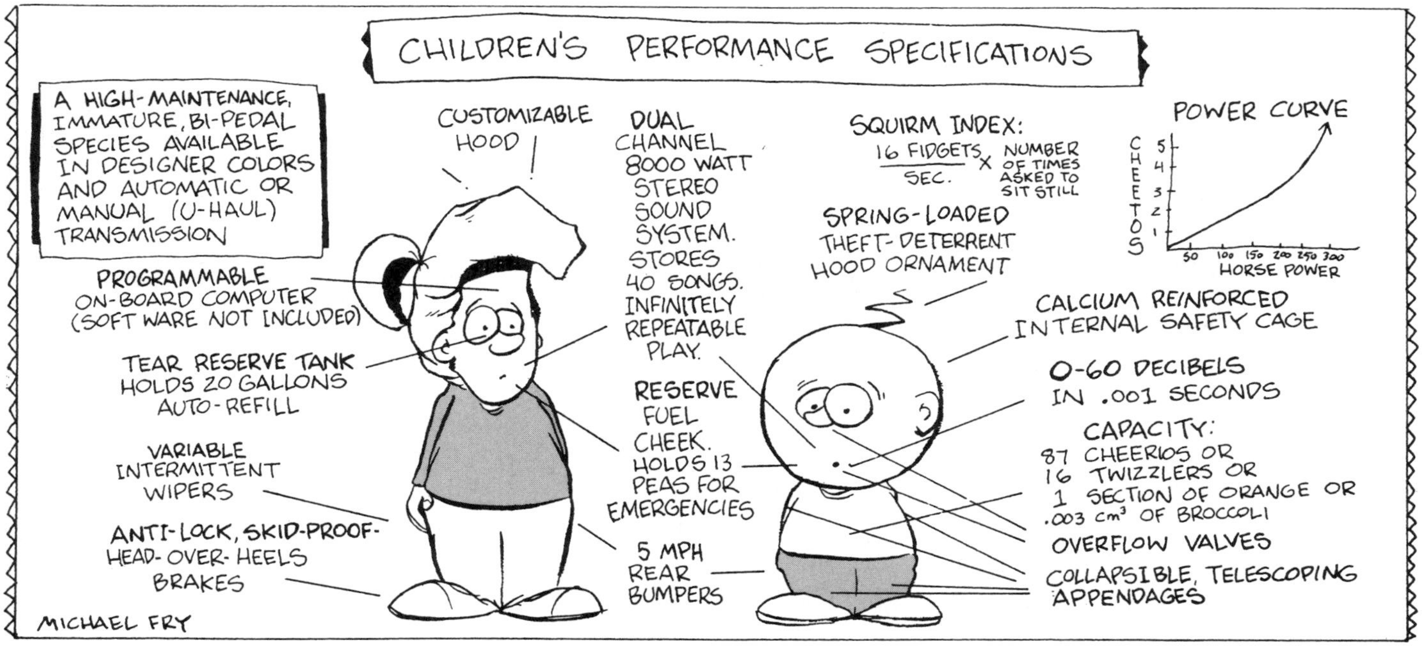

CHILDREN'S PERFORMANCE SPECIFICATIONS

A HIGH-MAINTENANCE, IMMATURE, BI-PEDAL SPECIES AVAILABLE IN DESIGNER COLORS AND AUTOMATIC OR MANUAL (U-HAUL) TRANSMISSION

CUSTOMIZABLE HOOD

DUAL CHANNEL 8000 WATT STEREO SOUND SYSTEM. STORES 40 SONGS. INFINITELY REPEATABLE PLAY.

SQUIRM INDEX: 16 FIDGETS / SEC. X NUMBER OF TIMES ASKED TO SIT STILL

POWER CURVE

CHEETOS 5 4 3 2 1

50 100 150 200 250 300 HORSE POWER

SPRING-LOADED THEFT-DETERRENT HOOD ORNAMENT

PROGRAMMABLE ON-BOARD COMPUTER (SOFT WARE NOT INCLUDED)

CALCIUM REINFORCED INTERNAL SAFETY CAGE

TEAR RESERVE TANK HOLDS 20 GALLONS AUTO-REFILL

0-60 DECIBELS IN .001 SECONDS

RESERVE FUEL CHEEK. HOLDS 13 PEAS FOR EMERGENCIES

CAPACITY: 87 CHEERIOS OR 16 TWIZZLERS OR 1 SECTION OF ORANGE OR .003 cm³ OF BROCCOLI

VARIABLE INTERMITTENT WIPERS

OVERFLOW VALVES

ANTI-LOCK, SKID-PROOF-HEAD-OVER-HEELS BRAKES

5 MPH REAR BUMPERS

COLLAPSIBLE, TELESCOPING APPENDAGES

MICHAEL FRY

DO YOU REMEMBER THE DAY WE MET?

LIKE IT WAS YESTERDAY!

IT WAS A THURSDAY.

IT WAS A SATURDAY

IT WAS SUNNY.

IT WAS RAINING.

YOU WERE WEARING A BEIGE SWEATER AND JEANS.

I WAS IN A SUN DRESS.

YOUR HAIR WAS SHORT IN A BLUNT CUT.

IT WAS BRAIDED DOWN THE MIDDLE OF MY BACK.

AND WHEN YOUR HEAD TURNED AND OUR EYES LOCKED, A BRILLIANT LIGHT FROM ABOVE BATHED YOU IN A SHIMMERING SHOWER..

KINDA LIKE THE TRANSPORTER BEAM ON STAR TREK

YOU REMEMBERED!

WHEW!

MICHAEL FRY

HEY! I'VE GOT A GREAT IDEA! WHY DON'T WE PUT TOGETHER A JOURNAL!

YOU TELL ME WHAT HAPPENS EVERYDAY, AND I'LL WRITE IT DOWN.

SO, WHAT HAPPENED TODAY?

JIMMY THREW UP.

WELL... YES... BUT, I THINK WHAT I MEANT WAS, DID YOU LEARN ANYTHING?

TO GET OUT OF THE WAY?

NO, NO... I MEAN, HOW DID YOU FEEL ABOUT TODAY?

IT WAS GROSS?

SOMETHING ELSE MUST HAVE HAPPENED!

SALLY THREW UP, TOO.

NEVERMIND.

MICHAEL FRY

THE WORKING MOM TO-~~DO~~ ENDURE LIST

Monday May 1, 1995 — AM

1	DO HOUSEWORK.
2	PAY BILLS.
3	GO TO BED. MAKE LOTS OF NOISE SO SPOUSE KNOWS YOU'VE BEEN UP.
4	WAKE UP 4 TIMES FOR CHILD POTTY EMERGENCIES.
5	DREAM OF CLONING YOURSELF.
6	WAKE UP TO CAFFEINE-ADDLED D.J. PLAYING AEROSMITH. SHOOT RADIO.
7	AWAKEN TO PITTER-PATTER OF RAMPAGING ELEPHANTS.
8	NUKE BREAKFAST. TAKE COFFEE INTRAVENOUSLY. PLACE LUNCHABLES IN LUNCH BOXES.
9	REALIZE AT DAY CARE DROP-OFF THAT KIDS HAVE MIXED ANIMANIACS TOPS WITH LION KING BOTTOMS. SHRUG.
10	DRIVE TO WORK. SPILL COFFEE. RIP SUIT, RUN HOSE. TAKE PROZAC.
11	ARRIVE AT WORK. SURF THE NET. PLAY DOOM. FEEL BETTER.
12	EAT HUGE CARBOHYDRATE LUNCH ON PURPOSE.

Monday May 1, 1995 — PM

1	SLEEP AT DESK.
2	REALLY HOPING SPOUSE IS HAVING AS SPECIAL A DAY AS YOU ARE.
3	EXPERIENCE 12 MINUTES OF GENUINE PRODUCTIVITY.
4	MAKE TOMORROW'S TO-DO LIST.
5	PICK UP KIDS AT DAY CARE. OBSERVE STAFF. POINT AND SNICKER. SHRUG.
6	ARRIVE AT HOME. OBSERVE EMPTY FRIDGE. ORDER PIZZA. AGAIN.
7	PLAY WITH KIDS. BATHE KIDS. GIVE KIDS A TREAT. BATHE KIDS AGAIN.
8	PUT KIDS TO BED. READ "CURIOUS GEORGE" FOUR TIMES FROM MEMORY.
9	DO ALL THE WORK YOU DIDN'T DO TODAY.
10	WATCH KIDS SLEEP. SMILE.
11	WATCH SPOUSE SLEEP. FROWN.
12	PASS OUT.

MICHAEL FRY

TRACY EXPLAINS IT ALL FOR YOU

HOW DOES MILK GET FROM THE COW TO OUR TABLE?

FIRST, YOU GET SOME COWS...

THEN, THEY GIVE YOU SOME MILK...

WHIRRRR

THEN YOU GOTTA "PASTURIZE" IT.

THEN, YOU BUY IT AT THE STORE.

MILK: IT'S DULL... BUT A GOOD KIND OF DULL

THEN YOU TAKE IT HOME AND DRINK IT.

SLURP!

THEN YOUR SISTER DOES SOMETHING STUPID AND MAKES YOU LAUGH.

MMPH...

THEN MILK SHOOTS OUT YOUR NOSE...

...AND LANDS ON OUR TABLE.

THE END.

MICHAEL FRY

SAVE THE OVER-PROTECTED

HELLO, I'M JENNIFER

I'M SCOTT.

WE'VE ONLY EVER WATCHED PBS.

I'VE NEVER SEEN "ANIMANIACS"

ALL OUR TOYS ARE MADE IN SCANDINAVIA OF HAND-BURNISHED TEAK.

I'VE NEVER SEEN GACK.

WE ONLY EAT WHOLE-GRAIN, ORGANIC, HAND-BLOWN BARLEY PUFFS.

I'VE NEVER SEEN SUGAR.

NOW YOU HAVE THE OPPORTUNITY TO HELP THESE CHILDREN LEAD A MORE NORMAL LIFE. FOR ONLY PENNIES A DAY, YOU CAN BRING THEM ROCKY AND BULLWINKLE, FLOAM, AND FROOT LOOPS. PLEASE, ACT NOW...

...BEFORE IT'S TOO LATE.

I'VE NEVER SEEN A HAPPY MEAL.

SHUDDER

MICHAEL FRY

"PHYSICIAN, n, ONE UPON WHOM WE SET OUR HOPES WHEN ILL, AND OUR DOGS WHEN WELL." -AMBROSE BIERCE-

I NEED A C.B.C., I.V., L.M.N.O.P., AND A MILK BONE STAT!

DR. BOB →

THE CHILDREN'S DICTIONARY

Nap *n* /nap/ Forced sleep. A complete waste of quality play time. A widely recognized human rights violation. Cruel and unusual punishment. Solitary confinement. A fate worse than death. The end of time.
syn: **imprisonment** *ant:* **freedom**

Having exhausted her appeals, Tracy decides to serve her one **nap** *sentence in silent protest.*

"NO DAY IS SO BAD IT CAN'T BE FIXED WITH A NAP."
-CARRIE SNOW

HAS NEVER HAD A BAD DAY IN HIS LIFE →

"FOR FAST ACTING RELIEF TRY SLOWING DOWN."
-LILY TOMLIN

SUFFERS FROM TOO LITTLE STRESS →

A RECIPE FOR DISASTER

1 Exhausted Mother
1 Traffic Jam
1/1000 of a Tank of Gas
2 Starving Children
6 Peanuts

Combine ingredients and mix.
Place in preheated car.
Bake at 100° for 1 minute.
Unnerves 3.

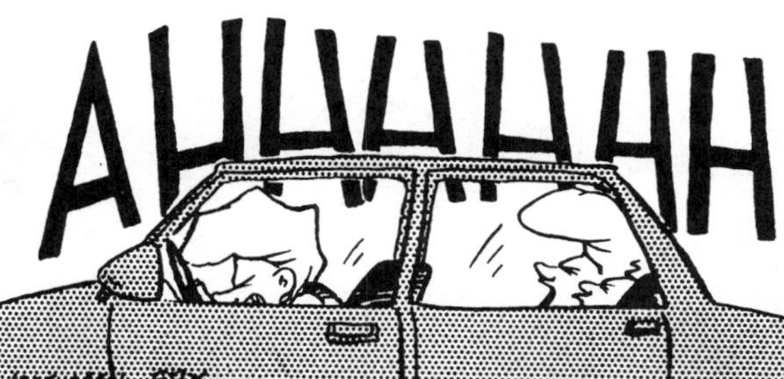

"IF YOU MEAN TO KEEP AS WELL AS POSSIBLE, THE LESS YOU THINK ABOUT YOUR HEALTH THE BETTER."
-OLIVER WENDELL HOLMES SR.-
BOB EATS TAKE-OUT
NUTRITION FACTS

Non-Nutrition Facts

Serving Size Approx. 2 lbs of Chocolate Morsels
Servings per Container 1

Amount Per Serving	Mix	With a Jolt Cola
Guilt	2000%lse*	2040%lse
Guilt from Enjoyment	1999%lse	2039%lse
	% Daily Value*	
Total Enjoyment 280s/s**	**3000%**	**3100%**
Smiles 1s/s	**1%**	**30%**
Grins 1s/s	**1%**	**30%**
Giggles 1s/s	**1%**	**30%**
Ecstatic Rapturous Moaning 277s/s	**2997%**	**2910%**
Mouth Feel 5043fg/lb***	**1600%**	**1602%**
Serotonin Boost 600038nt****	**8003%**	**8005%**
Self Respect 0lymm*****	**0%**	**0%**

*Percent lowered self-esteem. **Satiation per swallow
***Fat grams per taste bud. ****Neurons tickled.
*****Look yourself in the mirror in the morning.

MICHAEL FRY

?
ZIP!
WHY YOU CAN NEVER FIND YOUR KIDS' SHOES
THE RUNNING! THE JUMPING! THE DOUBLE-KNOTS! I CAN'T BREATHE!
RUN AWAY! RUN AWAY!
MICHAEL FRY

"WOMEN WHO SEEK TO BE EQUAL WITH MEN LACK AMBITION." -TIMOTHY LEARY-
THE LAST BASTION OF MALE DOMINATION
IT'S A FACT! WOMEN LACK THE UPPER-BODY STRENGTH TO LIGHT THE GRILL AND HOLD A BEER AT THE SAME TIME.
E-Z LIGHT CHARCOAL
MICHAEL FRY

THE DOG FORMERLY KNOWN AS BOB
FEED ME
HIS NEW SYMBOL
THIS IS HER NEW SYMBOL. FROM NOW ON SHE WANTS TO BE KNOWN AS THE CHILD FORMERLY KNOWN AS ZELDA.
MICHAEL FRY

WHILE ON SHORE LEAVE IN THE NAVY, BOB GOT A TATTOO ON HIS BUTT THAT SAYS...
Z
"...BORN TO NAP."
PARENT TATTOOS
SLEEP
CALL JOE
TAKE PROZ
TRACY
PIZZA 555-6832
CUPCAKES ZELDA WED.
DR. APPT 10:30 TUES.
DAYCARE 555-0123
EAT LUNCH
LOSE MIND
CALL MOM
RUN AWAY! RUN AWAY!
MICHAEL FRY

"CONFORMITY IS THE APE OF HARMONY"
-RALPH WALDO EMERSON-

WHAT WOULD YOU SAY IF I WERE TO LOSE 20 lbs., BULK UP AND GROW MY HAIR LONG?
NAHHHHH... YOU LOVE ME JUST THE WAY I AMMM!!
I HATE BILLY JOEL.
MICHAEL FRY

"ALL GOD'S CHILDREN ARE NOT BEAUTIFUL. MOST OF GOD'S CHILDREN ARE, IN FACT, BARELY PRESENTABLE."
-FRAN LEBOWITZ-
BOBIO

THE ANTI-BOB
AWAKE
ALERT
ROLLS OVER ON COMMAND
FORMER SLED DOG
JOGS

THE ANTI-BARBIE
PRACTICAL EASY-TO-CARE FOR HAIR STYLE
BRAIN
THICKISH GLASSES
LIP DE-GLOSS
FASHION BACKWARD
NIN
LITERATE
NO MALIBU BEACH HOUSE
ANKLES FUSED IN THE NORMAL POSITION
NO PINK VAN
NO KEN
SENSIBLE SANDALS
MICHAEL FRY

"THE WANT OF A THING IS PERPLEXING ENOUGH. BUT THE POSSESSION OF IT IS INTOLERABLE." -JOHN VANBRUGH-
I JUST FEEL SO... SO...
...DISNEY!
WE'RE VERY EXCITED. WE'RE THE FIRST ON OUR BLOCK WITH POCAHONTAS UNDERWEAR.
WHOA...
MICHAEL FRY

"TELEVISION IS FOR APPEARING ON, NOT LOOKING AT." -NOEL COWARD-
THIS PROGRAM IS CLOSED-CAPTIONED FOR THE HUMOR-IMPAIRED
HOW TO TEACH YOUR KIDS TO READ IN ABOUT 10 SECONDS
TURN ON LOONEY TOONS
CLICK
TURN OFF THE SOUND
ZING
TURN ON CLOSED-CAPTIONING
D-D-DAFFY D-DUCK EX-PL-PLODES...
B-B-BOOM!
MICHAEL FRY

WHAT YOUR DOG SAYS ABOUT YOU WHEN YOU'RE NOT AROUND
MY OWNERS? THEY'RE OKAY, EXCEPT FOR BEING ON THIS WHOLE DOMINANCE TRIP.
WHAT YOUR KIDS SAY ABOUT YOU WHEN YOU'RE NOT AROUND
AND THEN MY DAD FELL ASLEEP ON THE COUCH IN HIS UNDERWEAR... AND THIS LITTLE BIT OF DROOL FORMED ON HIS LIPS... AND HE STARTED, LIKE, BLOWING BUBBLES!
I KNOW... THEY'RE SO PRECIOUS AT THAT AGE.
MICHAEL FRY

BOB LISTENS TO THE CALL OF THE MILD
TAKE IT EASY, BOB... DON'T EXERT YOURSELF. HAVE A DONUT.
ROMULUS AND REMUS GET KICKED OUT OF DAY CARE
IT WASN'T THE BITING OR THE GROWLING OR EVEN THE HOWLING... BUT WHEN THEY ORGANIZED THE OTHER KIDS INTO A PACK AND SEPARATED POOR MRS. FINCH FROM THE OTHER TEACHERS, WELL...
PANT PANT PANT PANT PANT PANT PANT PANT PANT
MICHAEL FRY

"WHEN YOU'RE AN ORTHODOX WORRIER, SOME DAYS ARE WORSE THAN OTHERS."
-ERMA BOMBECK-

I WORRY ABOUT PEOPLE FINDING OUT ABOUT MY TAIL IMPLANT! WAIT!... OH, NO!

ARGHHHH

REALLY REALLY TRUE
STUFF

Barbie, Kelsey Grammer seen in Bayonne Lust Lounge

WORKING MOM SPONTANEOUSLY COMBUSTS

NEW SPON-COM DIET— IT WORKS!

"One second she was juggling career, family and a secret desire to run naked and screaming through the produce section... And the next second she was toast!"

MY TOENAILS TALK TO ME

I MARRIED A CANNED YAM

The rise and freefall of John Denver
"I'm now the guy in the purple dinosaur suit."

MICHAEL FRY

"IT IS THE GODS' CUSTOM TO BRING LOW ALL THINGS OF SURPASSING GREATNESS."

-HERODOTUS-

ACTUALLY, MY REAL NAME IS ZEUS... BUT YOU CAN CALL ME BOB.

"THIS IS GEORGE. HE LIVED IN THE ZOO. HE WAS A GOOD LITTLE MONKEY AND ALWAYS VERY CURIOUS." -H.A. REY-

HOW TO BE A KID
LESSON 1
WHERE TO HIDE THE PEAS
CHEEKS
PETS
BLEAH
POCKETS
MAYBE THEY'RE WATER SPOTS.
NO, THEY'RE PEAS.
CEILING
MICHAEL FRY

HOW TO BE A DOG
COCK YOUR HEAD TO ONE SIDE
PERK UP YOUR EARS
LOOK DESPERATE
BEG
THIS WILL GET YOU A PAT ON THE HEAD
YOU ARE NOW A DOG

" THE HARDEST THING IN THE WORLD TO UNDERSTAND IS INCOME TAX."
-ALBERT EINSTEIN
NUMBER OF DEPENDENTS? Ooo ...378 FLEAS.
NO, 379!
TICKS DON'T COUNT

If line 37 (taxable income) is -
And you are
At least
But less than
Comatose
Semi-Comatose
Fully Conscious
Working your butt off
Your tax is
0
∞
Ridiculous
Obscene
Sell the House
Sell the Children
AH, KIDS...?
BASS
100
MICHAEL FRY

AHHHYEEEEE I'M-INSAANE

INSIDE BOB'S STOMACH
FEED ME
NOTHING!
INSIDE YOUR KID'S STOMACH
I NEVER SAW A REQUISITION FOR THREE CHOCOLATE SUNDAES!
SEND 'EM BACK!
RECEIVING
MICHAEL FRY

THE PET POLICE
WHEN GIVEN THE COMMAND, "SIT," YOU TOOK A SEAT ON THE RECLINER!
SO?
THE PARENTING POLICE STRIKE AGAIN
YOU HAVE EXCEEDED YOUR CHILDREN'S NUTRITIONAL NEEDS FOR PIZZA FOR THE NEXT 60 YEARS.
MICHAEL FRY

"WOMEN ARE AS OLD AS THEY FEEL- AND MEN ARE OLD WHEN THEY LOSE THEIR FEELINGS." -MAE WEST-
MY BUTT'S ASLEEP...
I FEEL OLD.
WOMAN SHARING...
I FEEL LIKE OUR RELATIONSHIP HAS PLATEAUED. I NEED MORE ROMANCE. I NEED TO FEEL CLOSE. UNDERSTAND?
MAN SHARING...
WANNA SIP?
MICHAEL FRY

"A LOUD NOISE AT ONE END AND NO SENSE OF RESPONSIBILITY AT THE OTHER." -RONALD KNOX-
BOB
CRUELTY TO STUFFED ANIMALS
YOU SEE, TEDDY DOESN'T MIND SITTING ON THE POTTY...
THIS IS SO HUMILIATING...
MICHAEL FRY

AND FORTIFIED WITH THE MINIMUM DAILY REQUIREMENTS OF ACTUAL **FOOD!**

ONLY 93% SUGAR!

"WHEN I WAS A KID MY PARENTS MOVED A LOT – BUT I ALWAYS FOUND THEM."
-RODNEY DANGERFIELD-

TAKE A DEEP BREATH, TIGHTEN YOUR STOMACH, PULL FROM THE DIAPHRAGM AND SCREAM!

WHEN BARNEY MET BARBIE

HEY, BACKYARD GANG! TODAY'S SPECIAL WORLD IS "SHARING." CAN YOU SAY, "SHARING"?

RESIDUALS!

NO. THAT'S NOT QUITE IT.

" TO BE A SUCCESSFUL FATHER THERE IS ONE ABSOLUTE: WHEN YOU HAVE A KID, DON'T LOOK AT IT FOR THE FIRST TWO YEARS"
-ERNEST HEMINGWAY-

BOB'S DAD WAS A NOT-SO-GREAT DANE

KINDA AN OKAY DANE

LAZY? NO WAY. YOU'RE MATERNALLY CHALLANGED

Working Dad

HELPING OUT

HOW TO MAKE 60-40 SOUND LIKE 50-50

HOW TO TURN CHEERIOS AND TUNA INTO A NUTRITIOUS FOOD FEST
BOFFO GUY RECIPIES

GOLF WITHOUT GUILT
CALL IT A NATURE HIKE WITH THE KIDS

MICHAEL FRY

BOB'S WORST NIGHTMARE
SLEEPING BEAUTY'S EVIL FAIRY CASTS A SPELL ON ME AND...
I LIE AWAKE FOR A 100 YEARS!
...AND THEN SLEEPING BEAUTY PRICKED HER FINGER ON THE EVIL FAIRY'S SPINNING WHEEL AND FELL INTO A DEEP, DEEP SLEEP THAT LASTED 100 YEARS...
Sleeping Beauty
SIGH...
SHUDDER!
SHUDDER
Sleeping MOM
MICHAEL FRY

NICE HOUND OF HELL... NICE DOGGIE...
GRRRR...
THE MONSTER-UNDER-THE-BED CONVENTION
FRANK! LONG TIME, NO SEE! WHERE HAVE YOU BEEN HIDING?
I'VE RETIRED UNDER THE HIDE-A-BED. IT'S QUIET, AND I ONLY HAVE TO WORK SLUMBER PARTIES AND THE OCCASIONAL MOTHER-IN-LAW.
MICHAEL FRY

ME?... I FLOSS EVERY DAY!
SQUEEGEE... SQUEEGEE... SQUEEGEE...
THE TOOTH FAIRY'S LAMENT
SORRY IT'S ONLY A QUARTER, KID... AFTER THE NEW OSHA REGULATIONS FOR INFECTIOUS WASTE REMOVAL, YOU'RE LUCKY TO GET EVEN THAT!
BIO. HAZARD
BIO HAZA
MICHAEL FRY

"WE HOPE THAT WHEN THE INSECTS TAKE OVER THE WORLD, THEY WILL REMEMBER WITH GRATITUDE HOW WE TOOK THEM ALONG ON ALL OUR PICNICS." -BILL VAUGHAN-
COUGH IT UP! FAT BOY!
INVERTEBRATE DAY-CARE
AS A WORKING QUEEN WE KNOW HOW IMPORTANT IT IS FOR YOU TO KNOW THAT YOUR OFFSPRING ARE WELL TAKEN CARE OF. WE HAVE A TERRIFIC NURSE-TO-LARVA RATIO OF 400 TO 1! AND WE EVEN TAKE IN WINGLESS DRONES!
LARVA→PUPA→ADULT
KINDER-ANT ACADEMY
WAH! WAH! WAH! WAH! WAH!
MICHAEL FRY

"TELL THE TRUTH
BUT TELL IT SLANT"
-EMILY DICKINSON

LIES YOU CAN TELL YOUR KIDS ONLY ONCE

BRUSSELS SPROUTS?

THEY'VE GOT A TOOTSIE-ROLL CENTER.

MICHAEL FRY

I'M PLAGUED BY FEELINGS OF RESPONSIBILITY.
...I'VE BECOME CHRONICALLY DEPENDABLE...
...AND I HAVE ACUTE BOUTS OF TARIFTINESS.
HMM... HOW OLD ARE YOU?
35.
DO YOU DRIVE A MINI-VAN?
AH... YEAH.
MICHAEL FRY
DO YOU CHANGE THE OIL EVERY 3 MONTHS OR 3000 MILES?
YES!
DO YOU ROTATE THE TIRES?
YES!
DO YOU ALWAYS COME TO A FULL AND COMPLETE STOP?
OHMYGOD, YES!
YOU'VE GOT A BAD CASE OF **PREMATURE MATURITY**.
WHAT?!
IT'S CHRONIC. IT'S DEBILITATING. IT'S FATAL.
HOW LONG DO I HAVE?
ABOUT 50 YEARS.
I'M TOO YOUNG TO BE BORING!

A PARENT'S GUIDE TO COMMON HOUSEHOLD SOUNDS

THE SOUND OF A JELLY DONUT STRIKING A TV
FOAP...
MICHAEL FRY
THE SOUND OF A CHILD SLIDING DOWN THE HALL ON A FLOOR GREASED WITH BABY OIL.
SKOAM!
THE SOUND OF A DISCARDED PEA EXPLODING UNDER A BARE FOOT.
FWIRP!
THE SOUND OF A DOG BEING FORCED TO DRESS UP LIKE AUNT BEA IN HER SUNDAY BEST.
ELP!
THE SOUND OF YOUR COMPUTER DELETING CRUCIAL TAX INFORMATION TO MAKE ROOM FOR YOUR CHILD'S KID PIX CREATION
BRONG
THE SOUND OF BARBIE DISCOVERING THAT HER PINK VAN HAS BEEN RANSACKED BY TROLLS
DREEEK!
THE SOUND OF GOLF CLUBS BEING FLUSHED
WROSHKRBTXBLTTTT
YEEEE!

ONE PARENT'S DIRTY LITTLE SECRETS

YES, IT'S TRUE... I SECRETLY THROW OUT THE KIDS' HALLOWEEN CANDY WHEN THEY'RE NOT LOOKING.

I'VE NEVER BAKED A CUPCAKE IN MY LIFE. I SNEAK OUT AT NIGHT, BUY THEM AT THE STORE AND LATER CLAIM THEM AS MY OWN. PLEASE, DON'T TELL ANYONE.

NO... REALLY! I WAS UP ALL NIGHT!

I OVERSLEPT ONE MORNING AND SENT MY DAUGHTER TO DAY CARE WITHOUT HER LUNCH. I ENDED UP HAVING A PIZZA DELIVERED. NO, I'M NOT PROUD OF MYSELF.

PIZZA

I ONCE LET MY KIDS WATCH AN ENTIRE "GUMMI BEAR" MARATHON ON TV. I HOPE THEY CAN FORGIVE ME SOME DAY FOR DESTROYING THEIR ATTENTION SPANS.

BONK

OW!

ON PICTURE DAY AT SCHOOL I GAVE IN AND LET MY GIRLS DRESS AS NINJA BALLERINAS... GRANDMA NEVER SAW THOSE PICTURES.

I ONCE TOLD MY KIDS THAT LIMA BEANS WERE JUST GREEN M&M'S WITHOUT THE CHOCOLATE OR THE SUGAR...

YOU'RE **SURE** NO ONE CAN SEE ME?...

RELAX.

MICHAEL FRY

JOE, THIS IS AMY... SHE'S AN EXPERT IN MALE/FEMALE COMMUNICATION. SHE'S GOING TO TRANSLATE FOR US... READY?

I NEED MORE HELP AROUND THE HOUSE.

SHE NEEDS MORE HELP AROUND THE HOUSE!!

KIDS... COOKING... LAUNDRY...

KIDS! COOKING! LAUNDRY!

GOT IT?

GOT IT?

GOT IT.

HE UNDERSTANDS AND SYMPATHIZES WITH YOUR NEED FOR ASSISTANCE. HE WILL MAKE EVERY EFFORT TO COMPLY WITHIN THE LIMITS OF HIS GENDER.

MICHAEL FRY

GREAT.

GREAT!

GREAT.

FRIDAY EVENINGS EVERYWHERE ACROSS AMERICA

I'VE SEEN YOU BEFORE.

HAVE WE MET?

I THINK SO.

IT WAS ABOUT 11 YEARS AGO.

YES, IN A CLUB.

WE DANCED.

YOU STEPPED ON MY FEET.

I'M KNOWN FOR MY DANCING.

YOU SAID I HAD THE MOST BEAUTIFUL EYEBROWS YOU'D EVER SEEN.

I'M KNOWN FOR MY SWEET NOTHINGS.

AND THEN WE FELL IN LOVE, GOT MARRIED, HAD TWO KIDS AND TWO CAREERS...

AND WE NEVER SAW EACH OTHER AGAIN.

I **KNEW** I KNEW YOU.

NICE TO SEE YOU.

MICHAEL FRY

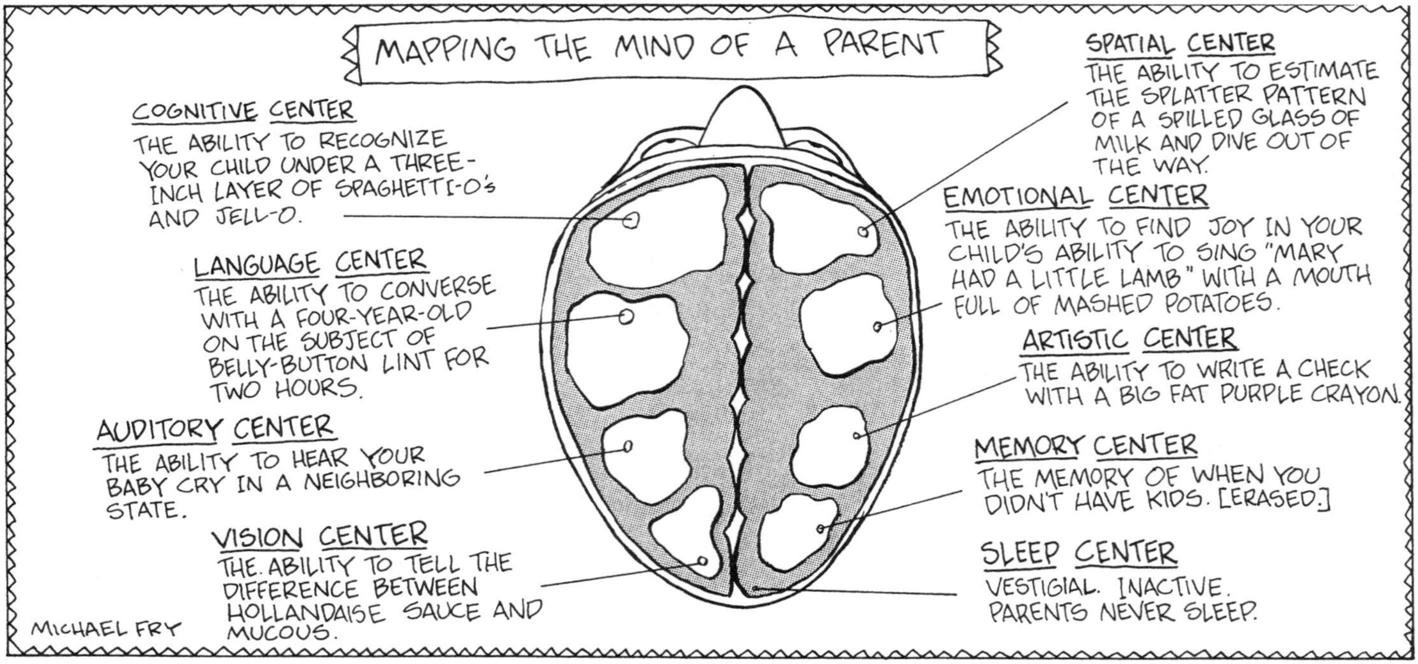

MAPPING THE MIND OF A PARENT

COGNITIVE CENTER
THE ABILITY TO RECOGNIZE YOUR CHILD UNDER A THREE-INCH LAYER OF SPAGHETTI-O's AND JELL-O.

LANGUAGE CENTER
THE ABILITY TO CONVERSE WITH A FOUR-YEAR-OLD ON THE SUBJECT OF BELLY-BUTTON LINT FOR TWO HOURS.

AUDITORY CENTER
THE ABILITY TO HEAR YOUR BABY CRY IN A NEIGHBORING STATE.

VISION CENTER
THE ABILITY TO TELL THE DIFFERENCE BETWEEN HOLLANDAISE SAUCE AND MUCOUS.

SPATIAL CENTER
THE ABILITY TO ESTIMATE THE SPLATTER PATTERN OF A SPILLED GLASS OF MILK AND DIVE OUT OF THE WAY.

EMOTIONAL CENTER
THE ABILITY TO FIND JOY IN YOUR CHILD'S ABILITY TO SING "MARY HAD A LITTLE LAMB" WITH A MOUTH FULL OF MASHED POTATOES.

ARTISTIC CENTER
THE ABILITY TO WRITE A CHECK WITH A BIG FAT PURPLE CRAYON.

MEMORY CENTER
THE MEMORY OF WHEN YOU DIDN'T HAVE KIDS. [ERASED.]

SLEEP CENTER
VESTIGIAL. INACTIVE. PARENTS NEVER SLEEP.

MICHAEL FRY

THE PARENTS BILL OF RIGHTS

YOU HAVE THE RIGHT TO USE SPIT AS A CLEANSING AGENT.

YOU HAVE THE RIGHT TO GO TO THE BATHROOM BY YOURSELF.

YOU HAVE THE RIGHT TO SAY, "BECAUSE I SAID SO."

WHY CAN'T I GROW UP TO BE A BEAUTY QUEEN?

BECAUSE I SAID SO.

YOU HAVE THE RIGHT TO BEGIN A SENTENCE WITH, "WHEN I WAS A KID..."

WHEN I WAS A KID, WE DIDN'T HAVE FOOD... WE ATE ROCKS AND DIRT AND STUFF.

YOU HAVE THE RIGHT TO SLEEP EXACTLY ONE HOUR A NIGHT.

WAHHHHHHHH

YOU HAVE THE RIGHT TO HIDE.

MOM? DAD?

YOU HAVE THE RIGHT TO PRETEND THAT YOU'RE A STRANDED ALIEN AND THE MOTHER SHIP WILL BE PICKING YOU UP ANY DAY NOW.

YOU HAVE THE RIGHT TO LIE TO UNSUSPECTING PARENTS-TO-BE.

PIECE-A-CAKE... NO SWEAT... THEY MAINTAIN THEMSELVES!

MICHAEL FRY

YOU HAVE THE RIGHT TO SCREAM.

A FEW EXCERPTS FROM THE COMMITTED BOOK OF CHILDREN'S WORLD RECORDS

TALLEST TALE TOLD AS A RESULT OF A BROKEN HEIRLOOM

IT WAS MR. ROGERS! HE'S TIRED OF BEING TYPECAST! HE WAS REHEARSING FOR HIS PART AS STANLEY IN "A STREET CAR NAMED DESIRE"

LONGEST PAUSE BETWEEN MINOR BOO-BOO AND ONSET OF CRYING

IT'S BEEN 35 MINUTES!

ANY SECOND NOW...

MICHAEL FRY

MOST CONSECUTIVE "WHYS"

WHY IS BARNEY PURPLE? WHY DOES DAD SHAVE HIS EARS? WHY CAN'T I HAVE A LEXUS? WHY ISN'T THERE A G.I. JILL? WHY ARE THE VEINS ON YOUR NECK BULGING? WHY? WHY? WHY? WHY?

SMALLEST POSSIBLE EXCUSE FOR NOT GOING TO SLEEP

MY TOENAILS ARE GROWING TOO LOUDLY.

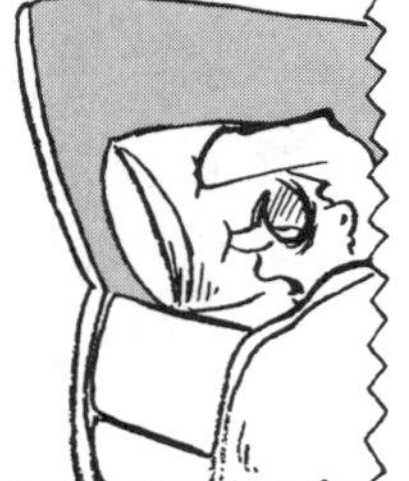

BIGGEST BALL OF DRIED PLAY-DOH

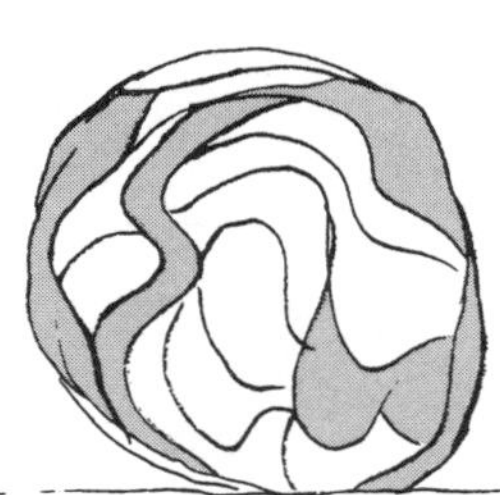

"PARENTS ARE SOMETIMES A BIT OF A DISAPPOINTMENT TO THEIR CHILDREN. THEY DON'T FULFILL THE PROMISE OF THEIR EARLY YEARS." -ANTHONY POWELL-

PARENTS EXPOSED!!
JOHNNY'S CLIFF
THIS IS THE CLIFF YOUR PARENTS ARE REFERRING TO WHEN THEY SAY, "IF JOHNNY JUMPED OFF A CLIFF, WOULD YOU JUMP OFF, TOO?"
THIS IS IT?!
WE'VE BEEN HAD...
MICHAEL FRY

WHY YES... MY NEW OFFICE DOES HAVE A WINDOW.
MICHAEL FRY

"THERE IS A HIDDEN FEAR THAT SOMEHOW, IF THEY ARE ONLY GIVEN A CHANCE, WOMEN WILL SUDDENLY DO AS THEY HAVE BEEN DONE BY." -EVA FIGES
THE GLASS DOOR
I CAN SEE THE POT ROAST, BUT I CAN'T GET AT IT

HOW TO BE A KID:
THE PROPER WAY TO EAT JELL-O
1.) MAKE IT DO THE "WATUSI."
BOBBLE... BOBBLE...
2.) SWISH IT BACK AND FORTH IN YOUR MOUTH
WROOOSH... SHROOOSH...
3.) SQUEEZE IT BACK OUT THROUGH YOUR TEETH
4.) RUN.
MICHAEL FRY

JELL-O FILLED
BLOPPADHA... BLOPPADHA... BLOPPADHA...

" I REALLY BELIEVE THERE ARE THINGS NOBODY WOULD SEE IF I DIDN'T PHOTOGRAPH THEM."
-DIANE ARBUS-
IT'S A SCRATCH! NOT A PICK! A SCRATCH!

THE PICTURES THE GRANDPARENTS NEVER SEE
MICHAEL FRY

"IF YOU HAVE ENOUGH FANTASIES, YOU'RE READY IN CASE SOMETHING HAPPENS."
-SHELIA BALLANTYNE-

"A BANK IS A PLACE THAT WILL LEND YOU MONEY IF YOU CAN PROVE THAT YOU DON'T NEED IT." -BOB HOPE-
VISA: IT'S NOWHERE I WANT TO BE.
ONE FOR THE BABY BOOK...
HER FIRST CREDIT CARD!
AND IT'S GOLD!!
MICHAEL FRY

BOB'S DAILY AFFIRMATION
I'M GOOD ENOUGH... I'M SMART ENOUGH... AND GOSH DARN IT, MY NOSE IS STILL WET!
WORKING MOM DAILY AFFIRMATION
I'M STILL HERE!
MICHAEL FRY

I'M WATCHING YOU WATCH ME WATCHING YOU WATCH ME WATCHING YOU WATCH ME...
CUT THAT OUT!
THE WORLD'S MOST POPULAR BABYSITTER
SHE'S HERE!
WHERE ARE THOSE LITTLE DARLINGS?
MICHAEL FRY

BRAIN WASH AND RINSE
FLIP
SCRUB SCRUB
YUP... SHE JUST NEEDS A NEW WASHER.
DRIP DRIP DRIP
MICHAEL FRY

" BETTER NEVER THAN LATE."

-GEORGE BERNARD SHAW-

THE CHILDREN'S DICTIONARY

Listen *v* /lis′ 'n/ 1.Selective hearing. 2.To pay attention to some sounds. 3. To be alert to catch an unexpected sound.
syn: **ignore** *ant:* **hyperfocus**

If they **listened** *very closely, Tracy and Zelda could hear the sound of the ice cream truck over all the background noise.*

"NO ONE REALLY LISTENS TO ANYONE ELSE AND IF YOU TRY IT AWHILE YOU'LL SEE WHY."

-MIGNON McLAUGHIN-

Grandparents

QUARTERLY Summer 1995

SPOILING GRANDKIDS

Go Ahead, They're Not Yours!

EASY GUILT-RIDDLED SUGGESTIONS TO GET MORE PICTURES, PHONE CALLS AND REQUESTS FOR ADVICE

HOW MANY GRANDCHILDREN ARE TOO MANY? 10? 20? 50?

WHAT EVER HAPPENED TO THANK YOU NOTES?

" WHY DO GRANDPARENTS AND GRANDCHILDREN GET ALONG SO WELL? THEY HAVE THE SAME ENEMY – THE MOTHER."

– CLAUDETTE COLBERT –

" YOU DO NOT LIKE THEM SO YOU SAY. TRY THEM! TRY THEM! AND YOU MAY. TRY THEM AND YOU MAY, I SAY." – DR. SEUSS.

BIG BAD BOB
MY, WHAT A BIG GUT I HAVE.
EVERY FAIRY TALE HAS TWO SIDES
AND THEN THE TRAGICALLY MISUNDERSTOOD WOLF SAID, "MY, WHAT A LIMITED UNDER-STANDING OF YOUR PLACE IN MY FOOD CHAIN YOU HAVE."
HEE-HEE
HEE-HEE
HEE-HEE
HEE-HEE
LITTLE RED RIDING HOOD REVISED
MICHAEL FRY

PING PONG PING PONG PING PONG PONG PING PING
WHERE ARE THEY NOW?
MR. MOOSE AND BUNNY RABBIT
After *Captain Kangaroo* was canceled in the early 80's, Mr. Moose and "Bun" became spokespuppets for the Ping Pong industry until the were replaced by Forrest Gump. These days they do mini-mall and laundromat openings with their old pal Dancing Bear and twice a year they headline with Andy Williams at his Branson, Missouri, theater.
MOON RIVER!!
MICHAEL FRY

WARNING TERRIBLE PUN AHEAD
GROAN
NO. IT'S JUST A SCRAPE. IT'S NOT THE "ELBOWLA" VIRUS.
MICHAEL FRY

AHHHHHHHH
THUNK!
WARNING: SECONDHAND SCREAMS MAY CAUSE CELIBACY IN CHILDLESS COUPLES
AHHHHHHHH
MICHAEL FRY

TEDDY BEARS ON THEIR NIGHT OFF

IF SHE SINGS "THE TEDDY BEAR PICNIC" ONE MORE TIME I'M GOING TO SCREAM!

HOW'D YOU LIKE TO SPEND THE WHOLE NIGHT IN A HEAD-LOCK?!

SHE DRAGGED ME ON MY BUTT ALL THROUGH SEARS... MY FUR IS NEVER GOING TO GROW BACK!

RAGGEDY ANN!... ANDY! DISCO DOWN!

MICHAEL FRY

"I LIKE TO GO TO MARSHALL FIELD'S IN CHICAGO JUST TO SEE HOW MANY THINGS THERE ARE IN THE WORLD I DO NOT WANT."

—MOTHER MARY MADELEVA

"I AM WORN TO A RAVELING."
-BEATRIX POTTER-
Z.
BOB'S DECADE OUT.
MOTHER'S DAY OUT
Tab
Cookies-n-Cream
Z.
MICHAEL FRY

"he was A Bear Of Very Little Brain."
-A.A. MILNE
A DOG OF EVEN LITTLER BRAIN
WHERE ARE THEY NOW
CHRISTOPHER ROBIN
He left The Hundred Acre Wood in 1963 to search the world for woozles. He and Piglet combed the seven continents but never were able to prove the existence of woozles. They thought they had one in Muncie, Indiana, but it turned out to be a bloated Shriner. Later they went back to England where the whole gang settled in Surrey and proceeded to gain a great deal of weight.
AYE, MATE! SEEN ANY WOOZLES?
MICHAEL FRY

"HOPE IS THE FEELING YOU HAVE THAT THE FEELING YOU HAVE ISN'T PERMANENT." -JEAN KERR
AND THEY ALL LIVED HAPPILY EVER AFTER -WITH DOGS.
FAIRY TALES FOR WORKING MOMS
ONCE UPON A TIME THERE WAS A LAND WHERE THE MEN TOOK THE INITIATIVE, THE CHILDREN LISTENED AND THE WORKING MOMS WERE WORSHIPED AS THE LIVING DEITIES THAT WE ARE.
MICHAEL FRY

TRAFFIC REPORTS FOR DOGS
THERE IS A 16-DOG PILEUP AT ELM AND 10TH AROUND A HYDRANT
TRAFFIC REPORTS FOR TELECOMMUTERS
THERE'S A ROLLERSKATE ON THE THIRD STAIR FROM THE BOTTOM, A MILK SPILL IN THE KITCHEN AND A JACKKNIFED FOUR-YEAR-OLD IN THE BATHROOM.
SCRATCH
YAWN!
SCRATCH
MICHAEL FRY

I WAS PATCHING THE ROOF WHEN ALL OF A SUDDEN EVERYTHING WENT BLACK.

DUCT TAPE CAN **FIX** ANYTHING

BARBIE'S HEAD WILL **NEVER** COME OFF AGAIN.

MICHAEL FRY

BOB IS DRESSED DOWN
GRRRR..
SUN DRESS →
DRESS-DOWN FRIDAY
FLING!
ZIP!
STREAK...
MICHAEL FRY

WATCH FOR FALLING BABIES
THE REAL REASON SHE WON'T GO TO SLEEP
...AND WHEN THE BOUGH BREAKS, THE CRADLE WILL FALL... AND DOWN WILL COME BABY, CRADLE AND ALL...
MICHAEL FRY

WHERE'S THE GUY WHO WROTE "IT'S A SMALL WORLD AFTERALL"?
A SPECIAL PLACE IN HELL
I MANUFACTURED JACKS... THE REALLY SPIKY KIND THAT PARENTS STEP ON IN THE MIDDLE OF THE NIGHT. YOU?...
I INVENTED THOSE BUTTON BOOKS... THE ONES WITH THE ANNOYING AND REPETITIVE SOUND EFFECTS.
MICHAEL FRY

"THE DIVINE RIGHT OF HUSBANDS, LIKE THE DIVINE RIGHT OF KINGS, MAY, IT IS HOPED, IN THIS ENLIGHTENED AGE BE CONTESTED WITHOUT DANGER." -MARY WOLLENSCRAFT
THE DIVINE RIGHT OF BOB →
Z
SHE MADE YOU SIGN A PRE-NATAL AGREEMENT?
IF I DON'T PERFORM 50% OF THE CHILDCARE DUTIES, SHE CAN OBTAIN A RESTRAINING ORDER THAT SAYS I CAN'T GET WITHIN 25 FT. OF THE REMOTE.
MICHAEL FRY

UNDER MY FUR, I'M A BRONZE GOD!

REALLY!

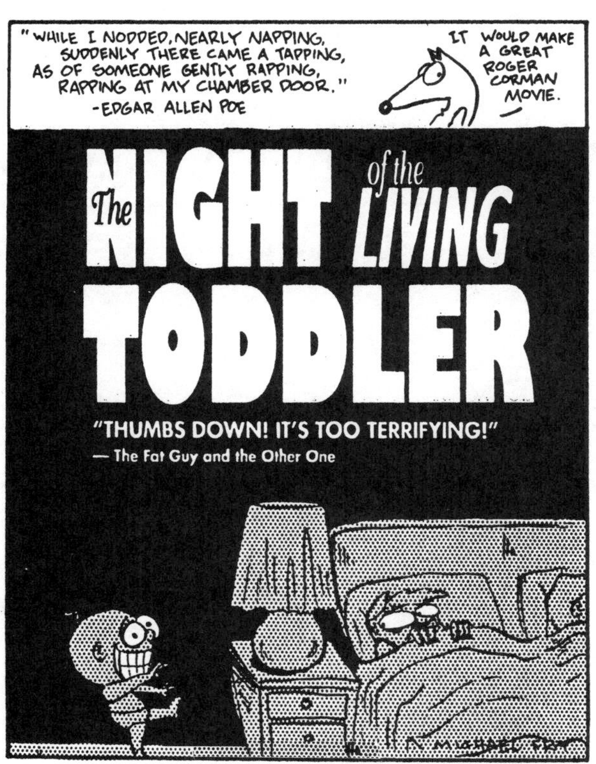
"WHILE I NODDED, NEARLY NAPPING, SUDDENLY THERE CAME A TAPPING, AS OF SOMEONE GENTLY RAPPING, RAPPING AT MY CHAMBER DOOR."
-EDGAR ALLEN POE
IT WOULD MAKE A GREAT ROGER CORMAN MOVIE.
The NIGHT of the LIVING TODDLER
"THUMBS DOWN! IT'S TOO TERRIFYING!"
— The Fat Guy and the Other One
MICHAEL FRY

SAFE, AFFORDABLE, QUALITY DOG CARE
THE VET
NO! NO! I WON'T GO!
THE SEARCH FOR THE MODERN HOLY GRAIL
WE'RE LOOKING FOR SAFE, AFFORDABLE, QUALITY CHILDCARE...
ME TOO!
WAHHH
MICHAEL FRY

"ON ONE THING PROFESSIONALS AND AMATEURS AGREE: MOTHERS CAN'T WIN."
– MARGARET DRABBLE
BEST IN SLOTH
THE MRS. AMERICA WORKING MOM PAGEANT
MY GOALS ARE TO SOLVE WORLD HUNGER... BRING PEACE TO MANKIND...
...AND TAKE A NAP.
SHE STOLE MY ANSWER!
MICHAEL FRY

"WE ARE NOT AMUSED."
-QUEEN VICTORIA
BOB'S SECRET
JOCKEY FOR ME!
WHAT POSSIBLE SECRETS COULD VICTORIA HAVE?
Sale THONGS Sale
Sale THONGS Sale
MICHAEL FRY

"ONE CAN NEVER CONSENT TO CREEP WHEN ONE FEELS AN IMPULSE TO SOAR."
-HELEN KELLER
BEEP BEEP
ZIP!
THERE'S SUCH A THING AS PROMOTING TOO MUCH SELF-ESTEEM
ZIP!
MICHAEL FRY

IT'S 11:00 AM HERE ON K-DOG AND IT'S TIME TO RISE AND SQUINT AND YAWN AND GO BACK TO SLEEP.
Z.
WREEEEEEEEEEEEEEE
HIT THE SNOOZE BUTTON.
Z.
SNOOZE
MICHAEL FRY

TWISTING THE NIGHT AWAY!
BUMP
TWIST
GRIND
TURN
CHUCK E. CHEESE SCHOOL
OKAY, WHEN THE ANIMATRONIC BAND PLAYS, WE TWIST! WE DON'T BUMP AND GRIND. WE DON'T SHAKE OUR BOOTY. WE DON'T GET DOWN! WE DON'T GET FUNKY! WE TWIST!!... YES?
CAN WE LAMBADA?
MICHAEL FRY

BARBIE'S HOT TUB
BOB
BUBBLE BUBBLE BUBBLE
BARBIES ON THEIR DAY OFF
THAT LITTLE BRAT HAD ME MODELING IN THE AQUARIUM AGAIN! A GUPPY ATE MY EYELASH.
I THINK JOE'S KINDA CUTE FOR AN ULTRA-VIOLENT ACTION FIGURE. HOW WOULD I LOOK IN FATIGUE CAPRI PANTS?
MY HAIR! MY HAIR!
MY HEAD! MY HEAD!
DRIP DRIP
MICHAEL FRY

IT'S A SIN!
IT'S A SIN!

DID YOU REMEMBER TO GET MY DE-WORMER?

HOW COME MEN NEVER GET CELL CALLS FROM THEIR FOUR-YEAR-OLDS IN THE MIDDLE OF IMPORTANT MEETINGS?

NO, HONEY... MOMMY DOESN'T HAVE TIME TO GUESS HOW MANY CHEERIOS YOU CAN STICK UP YOUR NOSE...

MICHAEL FRY

"...WHEN WE CHANGE WHAT WE BUY–AND HOW WE BUY IT–WE'LL CHANGE WHO WE ARE."

–FAITH POPCORN

" SLEEPING IS NO MEAN ART. FOR ITS SAKE ONE MUST STAY AWAKE ALL DAY."

– FRIEDRICH NIETZSCHE

THE DA VINCI OF SLEEP: SLEEPS ALL DAY AND ALL NIGHT.

"LET US ALL BE HAPPY, AND LIVE WITHIN OUR MEANS, EVEN IF WE HAVE TO BORROW MONEY TO DO IT." -ARTEMUS WARD
NO JOB. NO INCOME. $40,000 IN AVAILABLE CREDIT
JOE? HE'S OUT BACK SPLITTING A CORD OF CREDIT CARD APPLICATIONS FOR THE WINTER.
MICHAEL FRY

BOB'S TATTOO
HECK HOUND
KID TATTOOS
PEZ
MOM
MICHAEL FRY

YAWN
Ooo
IT JUST DOESN'T GET ANY DULLER THAN THIS.
TEA PARTY CONFIDENTIAL
THIS ISN'T TEA...THIS IS COLORED BATH WATER!
MY BUTT'S ASLEEP!
I'M SO BORED!
I GOTTA PEE!!
MICHAEL FRY

"MY WEAKNESS IS WEARING TOO MUCH LEOPARD PRINT." -JACKIE COLLINS
FAKE FUR
Vick's Secret
Not So Fashionable Underwear for Not So Fashionable Guys
THE MYSTERY IS YOURS TO KEEP...PLEASE!
VICK
THE MYLAR BIKINI BRIEFS ARE IN
3 FOR 1 ON SUPER SNUG THONGS
LONG JOHNS (WITH FEET) 1 ONLY
MICHAEL FRY

MORE INTERPRETATIONS OF SCREAMS

WAHHHHH
I AM NOT GOING TO SLEEP FOR THE REST OF THIS CENTURY

YOWWW
IF I EAT THESE LIMA BEANS MY BRAIN MAY MELT

MWAAAAA
YOU ARE IN MY SPACE

DOOOFF!!
I HAVE JUST DISCOVERED GRAVITY

NOOOOOO!
I ONLY HAVE ONE HAIR

SCREEECH!!
I JUST HAD THE REALIZATION THAT IT WILL BE 17 YEARS UNTIL I CAN DO ANYTHING I WANT.

WRUP!
MY HEAD IS STUCK IN A MARASCHINO CHERRIES JAR.

MICHAEL FRY

DAY CARE REPORT CARD

WHERE ARE THEY?
I LOST IT.
I ATE IT.

HEIGHTS DAY CARE

TRACY LARSEN
AGE: 4

H- HARVARD-BOUND
A- AVERAGE
S- SPEND THE COLLEGE FUND

Intellectual Development

MANIPULATING PARENTS H

KNOWING THE ENTIRE FOX LINEUP ON SATURDAY MORNINGS H

UNDERSTANDING THE UNIVERSE AND HER PLACE AT THE CENTER OF IT. H

Notes: Knows exactly how many seconds till Christmas

Emotional Development

MAKING NEEDS KNOWN USING LESS THAN 120 db H

DELAYING GRATIFICATION FOR MORE THAN 3 SECONDS H

Notes: A very fine whine! Admirable, yet annoying!

Physical Development

POSSESSING THE ENERGY EQUIVALENT OF A HYDROGEN BOMB H

SHOOTING MILK OUT HER NOSE FOR DISTANCE AND ACCURACY H

Notes: Works well with mud!

MICHAEL FRY

I'VE RUN A MARATHON

I'VE KAYAKED DOWN THE UPPER SALEK RIVER IN AUSTRIA AND TURNED OVER ONLY ONCE.

I STOOD ON THE ROOF OF A PARIS HOTEL AT MIDNIGHT AND KISSED A GIRL WHOSE NAME I DON'T REMEMBER.

I FOLLOWED THE GRATEFUL DEAD FOR THREE WEEKS IN '83 AND I REMEMBER ALMOST ALL OF IT.

I WROTE A SCREENPLAY THAT GOT READ BY THE GUY WHO LIVES NEXT DOOR TO THE GUY WHO CLEANS SPIELBERG'S POOL.

I HAVE NEVER LOST AT TRUTH OR DARE.

I MET MY WIFE, FELL IN LOVE AND SWORE AN OATH TO NEVER BE DULL.

MICHAEL FRY

AND NOW. HERE I AM...

... IN A WALMART...

145

146

THE RED ONE! THE RED ONE!

...BUYING A POTTY.

THAT ONE HAS A SPRING-LOADED LID!

A TIME MANAGEMENT ANALYSIS OF ZELDA'S DAY

SLEEPING

Z

16 HRS.

EATING

3 HRS.

SCREAMING

AHHH

2½ HRS.

DIAPER ABSORPTION TESTING

AHHHHHHHH

1½ HRS

TACTILE EXPLORATION

BLECK!

25 MIN.

ORAL EXPLORATION

MICHAEL FRY

20 MIN.

LAUGHING

HA

14 MIN.

WATCHING TV

NEXT ON "CROSSFIRE"!...

55 SEC.

SITTING AND CALMLY DOING NOTHING

TIME'S UP!

5 SEC.

INSIDE BOB'S HOUSE
THE EIGHT BALL IN THE CORNER POCKET...
WHACK! T-LUNK!
INSIDE THE TOY CHEST
YOU'RE TOUCHING ME!
YOU'RE TOUCHING ME!
HEY, BARBIE! PULL MY FINGER!
WHEN WAS THE LAST TIME YOU BRUSHED?
JACK! GET BACK IN YOUR BOX!
AIR! AIR! I'M CLAUSTROPHOBIC!
I'M FREE! I'M FREE!
MICHAEL FRY

"THE ONLY WAY NOT TO THINK ABOUT MONEY IS TO HAVE A GREAT DEAL OF IT." -EDITH WHARTON
BOB'S SAFE-DEPOSIT HOLE
MY PEDIGREE...
THEY FOUND THE COLLEGE FUND!!
MICHAEL FRY

DOGS WHO RUN WITH THE CARS
IT DIDN'T LOOK PARKED!...
WOLVES WHO RUN WITH THE WOMEN
I LIKE RUNNING WITH WOMEN... IT'S NOT LIKE IT'S A BIG CONTEST WITH THEM.
YEAH, THEY'RE NOT TRYING TO ONE-UP YOU ALL THE TIME.
WE COVER A LOT MORE GROUND!
AND AFTERWARDS, THEY SMELL A WHOLE LOT BETTER!
MICHAEL FRY

HI, HONEY, I'M HOME!... HONEY?... KIDS?... BOB?
Z Z Z Z
Working Mom
100 WORST COMPANIES FOR WORKING MOMS
WHY, YES, WE ENCOURAGE OUR EMPLOYEES TO SPEND TIME WITH THEIR FAMILIES
JUST NOT WHILE THEY'RE AWAKE...
DESAD TECH
MICHAEL FRY

THE ITSY-BITSY DAY CARE

ANY LATE PICKUP PENALTIES?

I EAT YOUR YOUNG.

MICHAEL FRY